EgyptAir
Weathering Storms

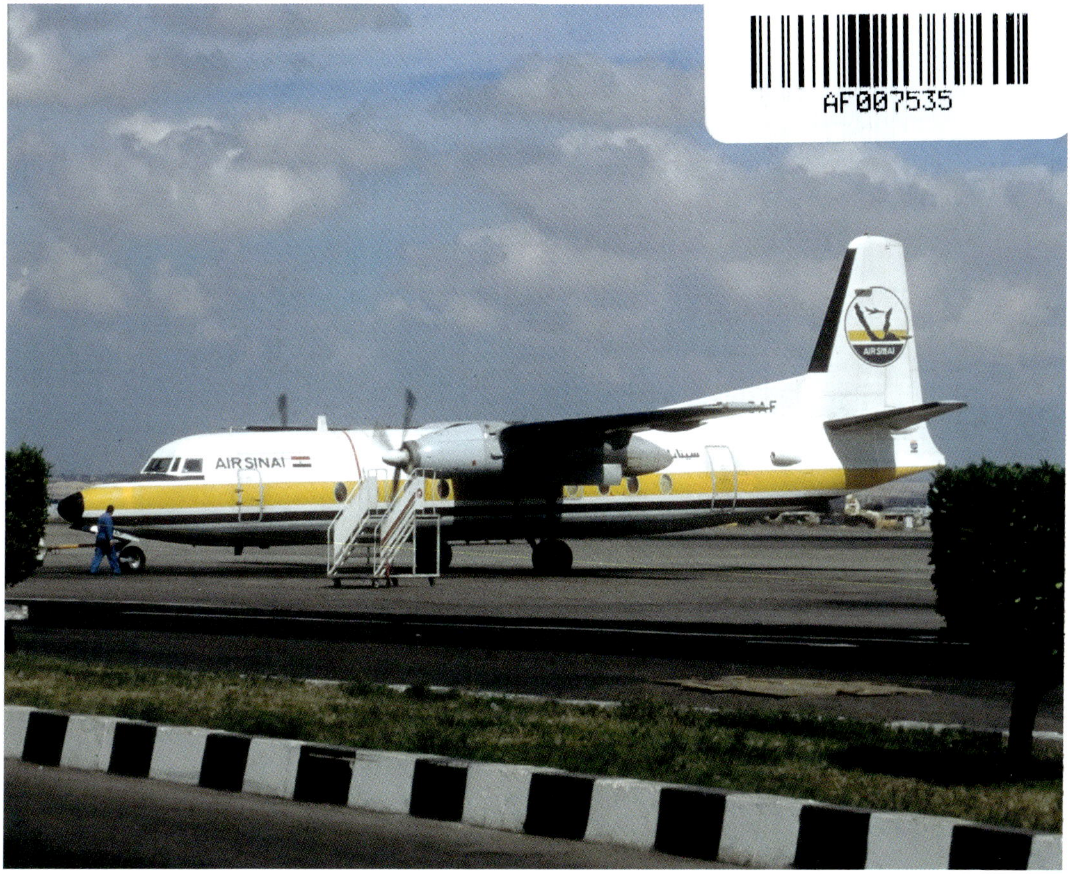

JOZEF MOLS

KEY Books

AIRLINES SERIES, VOLUME 14

Front cover image: An EgyptAir Boeing 787-9 at Paris Charles de Gaulle Airport. (Eric Salard, CC BY-SA 2.0, via Wikimedia Commons)

Title page image: After the peace treaty with Israel, EgyptAir set up a 'ghost airline' to operate flights between the two countries. (Jozef Mols)

Contents page image: During the Nasser regime, EgyptAir started to buy Russian-made jets like this Tupolev TU-154. (Alan Bushell)

Back cover image: EgyptAir Express Embraer 170-100LR. (Raymond Zammit)

Acknowledgements

I would not have been able to write this book without the help of many correspondents in Egypt and around the world and I am very grateful to them and to the libraries and research institutions that made their material available. I am also very grateful to all of the photographers who provided the images that illustrate this book. Special thanks go to my partner Marianne Van Leuvenhaege who encouraged me while researching this subject and writing the book, and who was my first proofreader. And of course, my gratitude also goes to Key for publishing and distributing this book.

Published by Key Books
An imprint of Key Publishing Ltd
PO Box 100
Stamford
Lincs PE9 1XQ

www.keypublishing.com

The right of Jozef Mols to be identified as the author of this book has been asserted in accordance with the Copyright, Designs and Patents Act 1988 Sections 77 and 78.

Copyright © Jozef Mols, 2023

ISBN 978 1 80282 385 1

All rights reserved. Reproduction in whole or in part in any form whatsoever or by any means is strictly prohibited without the prior permission of the Publisher.

Typeset by SJmagic DESIGN SERVICES, India.

Contents

Introduction 4
Chapter 1   Early Beginnings 5
Chapter 2   Misr Airwork 7
Chapter 3   Revolution 14
Chapter 4   United Arab Airlines 18
Chapter 5   Russian Planes 22
Chapter 6   An All-Boeing Fleet 26
Chapter 7   A 'Ghost' Airline 30
Chapter 8   The Achille Lauro Incident 37
Chapter 9   Expansion 41
Chapter 10   Restructuring 47
Chapter 11   Air Cairo 50
Chapter 12   EgyptAir Express 56
Chapter 13   Crisis 62
Chapter 14   Restructuring 68
Chapter 15   Fleet Renewal 70
Chapter 16   Profits? 75
Chapter 17   EgyptAir Today 79
Appendix 1 Incidents and Accidents 84
Appendix 2 EgyptAir Fleet Details 88
Appendix 3 Notes and References 90

Introduction

The origins of EgyptAir trace back to 1933 when Misr Airwork started operations. This private airline, set up by British and Egyptian investors, was intended to connect the major political and economic centres of Egypt with its neighbouring Arab countries. During the war years, the Egyptian government saw the need to take full control of the operations of the airline, which had strategic significance as a consequence of the bitter battles between former Allied and Axis forces in Egypt and Libya. In 1951, the government gained all of the shares in the airline, together with those of another private airline known as SAIDE, which had also been established. When President Nasser came to power in 1954, Egypt and Syria were merged to form the United Arab Republic: an experiment that lasted from 1958 until 1961. In that short time frame, the airline Misr was renamed United Arab Airlines and merged with Syrian Air. The Egyptian government would dominate the management of the new bi-lateral airline. Jets were introduced on routes linking Cairo with European and Arab capitals. Tourism was developing after the war years, and the airline tried to attract tourists to its home country, but was hampered in these efforts by wars between Arab states and Israel, as well as by revolutions in Egypt and neighbouring countries. When Nasser died in 1970, United Arab Airlines changed its name to EgyptAir following the country changing its name to the Arab Republic of Egypt.

EgyptAir faced the problems that once plagued United Arab Airlines. But each time, the airline managed to survive and even grow. The recent COVID-19 crisis affected EgyptAir and the Egyptian tourism sector, but the airline weathered the storm. The current war waged by Russia against Ukraine has also had a negative impact on tourism and air travel, but with the help of the Egyptian government, EgyptAir survives.

Jozef Mols
Wommelgem, Belgium
15 January 2023

Chapter 1
Early Beginnings

The creation of national airlines and their fortunes are influenced – if not dictated – by economic and political factors, as well as by technological evolution. Political, social, geographical, economic and cultural relations between neighbouring countries also play an important role.

It's more than 100 years since Egypt declared its independence from the British Empire and in that time the country has endured major political upheaval, wars with neighbouring countries and economic strife. European powers continued to retain power and dominance in the region, and the history of modern Egypt, up until recently, has been subject to control by European nations.

The first airline

Imperial Airways, the British government-owned airline, was the first airline to set up a trade route with Egypt after aviator Alan Cobham made a route survey flight from the UK to Cape Town and back in his de Havilland DH.50J floatplane between 16 November 1925 and 13 March 1926. The outward route was from London via Paris, Marseille, Pisa, Taranto, and Athens, to Solum in Egypt. Then the flight continued from Cairo to Luxor and Aswan in Egypt and to Wadi Halfa in Sudan. The route began service on 12 January 1927 using a DH.66 aircraft.

In 1929, Imperial Airways began its London to Karachi service consisting of a flight from London to Basle, a train to Genoa and a Short S.B. Calcutta flying boat to Alexandria, a train to Cairo and finally a DH.66 flight to Karachi.[1] These flights were intended to link the UK with overseas colonies in Asia and

EGYPT'S EARLY AVIATORS

In the early years of the 20th century young Egyptians, eager to train to become pilots, had to travel to France, Germany or the UK for their training. Ahmed Hassanein Pasha was such a pilot and a legendary figure in the history of Egyptian exploration of the Western Desert. He was one of the most powerful men in various governments under King Fouad and King Farouk and an adventurer at heart. It was his dream to fly from Egypt to London in a small plane. On his first attempt, he succeeded in flying over the Mediterranean, but crashed in southern France and his aircraft was destroyed. During his second attempt with a newly bought plane, he crashed in Switzerland. On his third attempt, he crashed in Italy and was seriously injured. He survived and made a fourth endeavour to fly to Europe. Half an hour before he was due to take off, a technician boarded the plane to do a final check of the instruments and five minutes later, the plane turned into a ball of fire. Hassanein's plane had been named 'Faiza' after one of King Fouad's daughters.[2]

'Faiza' was the name of another plane flown by Mohamed Sedki, the 'Egyptian Eagle'. Sedki set out to fly from Berlin to Egypt on 25 January 1930, and he arrived one day later. This day – 26 January – is celebrated as Egypt's National Civil Aviation Day. Sedki's plane was powered by a 40hp engine and weighed just 250kg (551lb). Sedki's succesful flight was a sensation and thousands of people cheered him on at Heliopolis Airport where a model plane made of flowers awaited him. King Fouad awarded Sedki with a Gold Medal of Excellence for his services to the nation. His success resulted in the establishment of the first Egyptian aviation club in Cairo.[3]

Between Sedki's solo flight in 1930 and 1933, a total of 33 male pilots graduated from Egypt's newly established school of aviation. Graduate number 34 was Lotfia Al-Nadi, the first Egyptian woman aviator to earn a pilot's licence.[4]

South Africa, and Egypt was a convenient location to stop between desinations. At the same time such stop-overs continued to mark the British presence in Egypt.

Establishing an airfield

Organising civil aviation requires the availability of airfields. Heliopolis Airport existed but could not be used by civilians as it served the British air force. Back in 1906, the Belgian industrialist Edouard Empain had bought 25sq km (9.65sq miles) of desert on which he planned to build a modern suburb devoted to luxury and pleasure, mainly intended for wealthy Europeans. The exotically styled 'Oasis of Heliopolis' had a golf course, amusement park, sports stadium, a horse racing course, electric lighting and two luxury hotels and was connected to the city centre of Cairo by an electric railway. Eager to promote his project, Empain organised an aviation meeting in cooperation with the Egyptian Tourism Association, the French 'Ligue National Aérienne' and the Aéro-Club de France. Several European pilots participated in this meeting, which was the first aviation meeting in an African country.[5]

During World War One, the aerodrome built by Empain for the aviation meeting, would be operated by the British Royal Flying Corps. In the 1920s it was named Almaza Airport, and later still, it became the first base of the Egyptian Army Air Force.[6] By the early 1930s, the Almaza Airport was fully managed by the Egyptians, and was the obvious choice for Egyptian civil aviators to select as a base.

Chapter 2
Misr Airwork

With the availability of Almaza Airport near Cairo, a group of trained pilots and an aviation club, all the ingredients were in place to start up an Egyptian airline. There were many good reasons to do so. The most obvious one was the establishment of an Arab airline in Egypt to take advantage of the strategic position of Cairo as a crossroad between the colonial powers at that time and the Middle East, Pakistan, India and the Far East. With an Italian presence in Libya and Tunisia, the establishment of an Egyptian airline could potentially counter any attempt by Mussolini to establish a joint Italo-Egyptian airline and further augment his footprint in North Africa.

When looking for a suitable partner to set up an Egyptian airline, Imperial Airways was not going to be acceptable. The company was the airline arm of the British Foreign Office and tainted by association with the British government. Instead, the British airline Airworks was selected for its political independence.[1] Alan Muntz was the chairman of Airworks, which provided aircraft on charter work.

On 7 May 1932, Misr Airways was established as 'Société Anonyme Misr Airwork' with an initial capital of 20,000 Egyptian pounds, provided by Banque Misr (85 per cent): hence the name 'Misr Airworks'. Airworks obtained ten per cent of the shares with the remaining five per cent in the hands of Egyptian private interests. Talaat Harb, a famous Egyptian nationalist and industrialist with great influence in local politics, was the major private shareholder. Shortly after the establishment of Société Anonyme Misr Airwork, a subsidiary was set up under the name of Misr Airlines. The airline was granted a 30-year concession from the Egyptian government and would receive subsidies for the first 15 years of operation. After that period, it would receive a monopoly on selected domestic routes.

Operations started in July 1933 from Cairo to the port city of Mersa Matruh via Alexandria with a fleet of two de Havilland DH84 Dragons (SU-ABH and SU-ABI). In December of the same year, a twice-weekly route from Cairo via Assiut and Luxor to Aswan was inaugurated. In 1934, the airline launched its first international flights to Lydda and Haifa in Palestine on a twice-weekly basis. It was a success, and the frequency was increased to daily flights in 1935. That year, flights to Cyprus from both Cairo and Port Said were introduced: first on a seasonal basis. Later when the route became very popular, it would run daily. In order to meet the expansion of the route network, a third Dragon Rapide was obtained, followed by a de Havilland DH 86 Express (SU-ABN) in June 1935. Another four de Havilland DH 89 Dragon Rapides (SU-ABP, SU-ABR, SU-ABQ and SU-ABS) were added later that year. By the end of 1935, the airline had carried 6,990 passengers, as well as 21,830kg (48,130lb) of cargo, flying 675,067km (419,467 miles).[2] A year later, another de Havilland DH 90 Dragonfly was added to the fleet. In 1936, the network expanded further with the addition of two weekly flights to Baghdad via Cyprus and Haifa. By 1936, the number of passengers had increased to 15,710. Misr Airlines added flights to Jeddah and Medinah, in Saudi Arabia, to its schedule, becoming the first airline in the world to serve both cities. In order to further realise its international ambitions, Misr Airlines signed a pool agreement with the Greek airline Société Héllénique de Communications Aériennes (SHCA). According to the agreement, Misr would carry passengers to Crete on the Cairo-Alexandria-Megalokastron route. Once in Crete, passengers could continue their journey to Athens and Salonika on SHCA aircraft. This service started in April 1939 with three services a week and ended in November 1940 following the invasion of Greece by the Axis powers.[3]

In September 1939 – after the German invasion of Poland – the Egyptian government took over all the airline's routes. The intention was to continue offering civilian air transport but at the same time to exercise military control over the airline. In 1940, Misr started a service to Beirut, Palestine and Adana. Notwithstanding the war in Europe, Misr transported some 22,872 passengers in 1941. During the course of the rest of the war, routes were opened to Khartoum and Damascus. In 1944, the airline obtained three Avro Ansons to be used for civilian transport. By the end of the war, the fleet stood at three DH89A Rapides, two DH89A Dominies, four DH86 Express, one DH84 Dragon, one DH90 Dragonfly and three Avro Ansons.[4] The carrier benefited from the Allies' regional aircraft disposal station based in Egypt that sold surplus aircraft. This way, five Beech C-45s, four de Havilland DH89s and two North American Texans (for training purposes) could be obtained. Two more Beechcraft D-18s were added in 1947, but these were delivered directly from the factory.[5] In 1948, the airline also obtained some second-hand Vickers Viking 1Bs. These were ex Aer Lingus, DDL and British European Airways. It was clear that the financial burden of the rapidly expanding fleet could not be carried by private investors alone. Therefore, the Egyptian government acquired the airline in May 1949 and changed its name to Misrair SAE.[6] With the fresh capital from the government, Misrair could further expand and the airline obtained three Sud-Est SE161 Languedoc aircraft in 1950. These were intended for deployment on longer routes and would replace the Vikings on routes to Geneva, Khartoum and Tehran.[7] This way, the airline was in a pole position to embark into a vast expansion plan. By December 1950, Misrair spread its wings to Geneva, Karachi and Addis Ababa. In April 1952, Kuwait, Athens, a direct flight to Baghdad, Port Sudan, Jerusalem and Aden were added to the route network, but services to Dhahran, Addis Ababa and Karachi were cancelled. The route to Geneva was extended to include Paris and was operated by Languedocs.[8]

In the meantime, Misr Airlines had lost its monopoly. In 1947, another Egyptian airline was set up by Misr Bank and King Farouk's family (55 per cent shares) and Italian interests. (45 per cent shares). On the Italian side, the Fiat conglomerate was the largest investor. Logically, the new airline – Services Aériens Internationaux d'Egypte or SAIDE – started out with a fleet of three Fiat G.212 aircraft. It also added three Savoia-Marchetti SM.95 aircraft with 38 seats to its fleet.[9] The first flights linked Cairo via Alexandria with Athens and Rome. In the summer of 1949, this route was extended to include Paris. The same year, a route to Italian Libya was opened from Cairo via Alexandria to Benghazi and Tripoli. In 1950, the route to Paris also included a stop-over in Milan. And finally, the route to Libya was extended to include Tunis. In April 1951, a route to Germany was opened with stops in Rome, München and Frankfurt. Also Beirut was added to the network. In July 1951, the Egyptian government took over all shares, previously held by Fiat. SAIDE became a fully Egyptian-owned airline. Notwithstanding this government intervention, SAIDE remained loss-making. In 1952, the airline was taken over by Misrair. Only the successful route Cairo-Tunis was carried over to Misrair's own route network. All other loss-making flights were cancelled.[10]

An early Misr Airlines poster. (Collection Jozef Mols)

De Havilland DH89 SU-ABU 'Heliopolis' at the Tel Aviv Airport. (Library of Congress, Washington D.C.)

Right: Misr Airlines 'Heliopolis'. (Library of Congress, Washington D.C.)

Below: A Misr Airlines de Havilland DH89 at Lydda Airport in front of a Palestine Airways Ltd Shorts Scion. (Library of Congress, Washington D.C.)

Above left: A Misr advertisement published shortly before World War Two. (Collection Jozef Mols)

Above right: An old Misr Airlines' poster. (Collection Jozef Mols)

Left: The 1935 Misr Airlines' timetable. (Collection Jozef Mols)

Misr aircraft at Cairo airport. (Willem van de Poll Collection, Nationaal Archief Den Haag)

Right: A Misr Beechcraft D-18S was used shortly after World War Two. (Collection Ed Coates)

Below: Misrair obtained ten Vickers Vikings. (Collection of Peter Keating via Alan Bushell)

From the EgyptAir archives, a Misrair Languedoc. (EgyptAir)

SAIDE used the SM.95 on domestic and international routes. (Collection Ed Coates)

Right: An old SAIDE poster. (Collection of Jozef Mols)

Below: Besides passengers and freight, SAIDE also transported airmail. (Collection Jozef Mols)

Chapter 3
Revolution

While Misrair was spreading its wings, the Arab world – its main market – was in turmoil. On 30 November 1947, the United Nations voted UN Resolution 181, which adopted the Partition Plan for Palestine, dividing the territory into Jewish and Arab sovereign states besides an international Jerusalem. The Partition was accepted by the Jewish leadership, but rejected by Palestinian Arabs and the Arab States. A 'civil' or 'ethnic' war between Jewish and Palestinian Arab militias was the result. Characterised by guerilla warfare and terrorism from both sides, it escalated at the end of March 1948 when the Jews went on the offensive and defeated the Palestinians in major campaigns and battles, establishing clear frontlines. During this period, the British maintained a declining rule over Palestine, but their mandate was terminated at midnight on 14 May 1948.

On that day, the last British troops left and the Jewish leadership in Palestine declared the establishment of the State of Israel.[1] This was followed, the next day, by the invasion of Palestine by the surrounding Arab armies and expeditionary forces and marked the beginning of the second phase of the war. In 1949, Israel signed separate armistices with Egypt on February 24, with Lebanon on March 23, with Transjordan on April 3, and with Syria on July 20. During this period the expulsion of the Palestinian Arabs continued. During the war, around 700,000 Palestinian Arabs were displaced either to the Palestinian territories captured by Egypt and Jordan, or to surrounding Arab states. Many of them would remain stateless in refugee camps.

Disappointed with the outcome of the war between Israel and the Arab countries, as well as with Britain's influence in Egyptian politics and economics, a group of Egyptian army officers formed the Free Officers Movement, led by Muhammed Naguib and Gamal Abdel Nasser. This movement was initially backed by both the Soviet Union and the United States of America. On 23 July 1952, the Free Officers deposed the pro-British Egyptian government of King Farouk whom the military blamed for Egypt's poor performance in the war with Israel, and a lack of progress in fighting poverty, disease and illiteracy in Egypt. With the departure of King Farouk, most British influence in Egypt disappeared. After a brief experiment in civilian rule, the Free Officers abrogated the 1953 constitution and declared Egypt a republic on 18 June 1953. Muhammad Naguib, a well-respected war hero, became the country's first president. Within six months, all civilian political parties were banned and replaced by the Liberation Rally government party. In 1954, the Muslim Brotherhood organization was outlawed. The same year, Gamal Abdel Nasser became prime minister and chairman of the Revolutionary Command Council (RCC).[2] While the Free Officers had, initally, acted to free their country from British domination, which had been exercised via a corrupt king and his court, they simultaneously tried to secure the independence of Sudan, which was also governed as a condominium of Egypt and the United Kingdom. The Egyptian revolutionaries – backed by the USSR and the USA – were faced with immediate threats from European colonial powers, particularly the United Kingdom (which had occupied Egypt since 1882) and France. Both nations were both wary about rising nationalist sentiment in territories under their control throughout Africa and the Arab world.[3] They severed the ties with Egypt and as a direct consequence, Misrair's right to fly to the UK and France was cancelled. The largest Arab airline at that time, spanning its wings to three continents, would soon be reduced to a small regional carrier. Nevertheless, the company ordered three Vicker

Viscounts in 1954: the year in which it carried 64,539 passengers.[4] As the operation of international routes had become problematic, Misrair developed its regional services by adding Benghazi, Tripoli and Tunis to its schedule and reinstating flights to Jerusalem, Baghdad, Port Sudan and Jeddah, using its fleet of Vickers Viking and the one remaining Languedoc aircraft. (Previously, in 1951 and 1952, the two other Languedocs had crashed). In 1955 – and notwithstanding the Western boycott – the airline carried 77,050 passengers.[5]

In the meantime – in 1954 – Nasser's popularity had grown tremendously, allowing him to dismiss Naguib from office and place him under house arrest. Meanwhile, the RCC managed to remain united in its opposition to the British and French, specifically in regard to the Suez Canal. Despite continued calls from the RCC, in debates in the United Nations, and pressure from both the USA and the Soviet Union, the British refused to transfer control of the Canal to the new regime. As a result, the RCC sponsored attacks on the British and French in the Suez Canal Zone.

On 26 July 1956 in a speech in Alexandria, Nasser announced the nationalisation of the Suez Canal. All assets of the Suez Canal Company were frozen and stockholders would be paid the price of their shares according to the day's closing price on the Paris Stock Exchange. The same day, Egypt closed the canal to Israeli shipping. Both the French and British – shareholders in the Canal – wanted Nasser removed from power. Israel wanted to reopen the canal to Israeli shipping, and at the same time saw an opportunity to strenghten its southern border and to weaken a dangerous and hostile state in a possible outbreak of war between Egypt with France and the UK. In a concerted move between Israel, France and the UK, an attack on the Canal Zone and on Egyptian territory was launched. The United States, although opposed to the continued presence of the colonial powers in the Middle East, could hardly intervene. The Americans were dealing with the near-simultaneous Hungarian Revolution. Vice-President Richard Nixon later explained: 'We could hardly complain about the Soviets intervening in Hungary and approve of the British and the French picking that particular time to intervene against Nasser. Besides, President Roosevelt was afraid that any American support for the French-British intervention might result in a backlash in the Arab world, which might win the Arabs over to the Soviet Union. Russian prime minister Nikolai Bulganin threatened to intervene on the Egyptian side, and to launch rocket attacks on Britain, France and Israel. In order to stop the war, the United States put pressure on the UK to end the invasion. Because the Bank of England had lost large amounts of money between 30 October and 2 November and Britain's oil supply had been restricted by the closing of the Suez Canal, the British had to ask for assistance from the International Monetary Fund. This assistance was denied following an American veto. In concert with American sanctions, Saudi Arabia started an oil embargo against Britain and France. Also NATO-member countries refused to sell oil to the UK and France. As a result, Egyptian sovereignty and ownership of the canal was confirmed by the United States and the United Nations, which resulted in an even greater popularity of President Nasser in his own country and other Arab states. During the war, however, Misrair had lost several of its aircraft, which were destroyed on the ground by Israeli, British and French warplanes. And of course, a series of regional services had to be suspended. But above all, the political volatility of the region would continue to influence Misrair's management for several decades to come.[6]

Fortunately, several reforms by the Nasser government had improved the economic situation in Egypt. Prior to these reforms, less than 0.5 per cent of Egyptians had owned more than one-third of all fertile land in the country. Due to the reforms, a law prohibited ownership of large parts of land, limited the rental rate for land, established cooperatives for farmers and set minimum wages. During the presidency of Nasser, cultivated land in Egypt increased by almost one-third. The middle class was growing and Egypt's economy grew at an average rate of nine per cent per annum for almost a decade. The share of manufacturing to Egypt's GDP rose from around 14 per cent in the late 1940s to 35 per cent by the early 1970s. The combination of the land-reform programme and the creation of the public sector in Egypt resulted in around 75 per cent of Egypt's gross domestic product being transferred from the hands of the country's rich, either to the state, or to millions of small owners and members of the middle class.[7] This positive evolution made it possible for Misrair to survive. The airline bought new Vickers Viscount aircraft, which were put into service in March 1956. In the meantime, Misrair had obtained second-hand Douglas DC-3 aircraft while waiting for the delivery of the Viscounts.

A Misrair timetable from 1955. (Collection Jozef Mols)

Right: A Misrair ticket from 1955. (Ashashyou CC BY-SA 3.0, via Wikimedia Commons)

Below: Misrair ordered Vickers Viscounts, which were later integrated into United Arab Airlines' fleet. (Collection Jozef Mols)

Bottom: A Misrair Vickers Viscount ordered when the name change to United Arab Airlines was pending. (Collection Jozef Mols)

Chapter 4
United Arab Airlines

Gamal Abdel Nasser had become a figurehead on the international scene: an image strenghtened by the outcome of the Suez crisis. In 1961, he became one of the leaders of the Non-Aligned Movement, a forum of 120 countries that were not formally aligned with or against any major power bloc. The movement had originated in the aftermath of the Korean War, as an effort by some countries to counterbalance the rapid bi-polarisation of the world during the Cold War whereby two major powers had formed blocs and embarked on a policy to pull the rest of the world into their orbits. The Non-Aligned Movement was formally established in 1961 as an initiative of the Yugoslav President Josip Broz Tito, Indian Prime Minister Jawaharlal Nehru, Ghanaian President Kwame Nkrumah, Indonesian President Sukarno and Egyptian President Gamal Abdel Nasser.[1]

On 1 February 1958, the United Arab Republic was established as a first step towards a larger pan-Arab state, originally being proposed to the Egyptian president by a group of political and military leaders in Syria. Pan-Arab sentiment had been traditionally very strong in Syria, and Nasser was a popular heroic figure. In mid-1957, Western powers had begun to worry about Syria's close relationship with the Communist world. Nasser was also afraid of a 'communist take-over' in the Arab world, and agreed on a total merger between his country and Syria. A plebiscite was held in Syria and Egypt on 21 February 1958 with Egyptians and Syrians voting in favour of the merger. Nasser was declared the first president of the United Arab Republic.[2]

Following the formation of the United Arab Republic, Syrian Airways merged with Misrair on 23 December 1958 to form United Arab Airlines. Syrian Airways had been established in 1946 with a fleet of two propeller aircraft with which it operated a domestic network. In 1947, three Douglas Dakota's had been obtained second-hand from Pan American World Airways, which had also provided technical assistance during the first years of operation of Syrian Airways. Later on, the airline had expanded its route network by adding regional destinations including Beirut, Baghdad, Jerusalem, Cairo, Kuwait and Doha. Financial difficulties and the 1948 Arab-Israeli War led to the withdrawal of Pan Am. In the mid-1950s, two Douglas DC-4/C-54 Skymasters, followed by a Douglas DC-4 were obtained.[3] Compared to Misrair – at that time the biggest airline in the Arab World – Syrian Airways was a dwarf. Therefore, its routes and equipment were absorbed by United Arab Airlines following the merger. By March 1960, the airline had 579 employees and a fleet of one Beechcraft D-18S, four DC-3s, six Vikings and six Viscounts. United Arab Airlines' timetable dated November 1959 showed new Vickers Viscount services to Athens, Geneva, Frankfurt, Kuwait, Damascus, Asmara, Benghazi, Tripoli and Jerusalem. Unfortunately, Aden ceased to be served altogether.[4]

On 9 June 1960, United Arab Airlines joined the jet-age with the delivery of its first de Havilland Comet 4C (SU-ALC). By October 1960, the airline had Comets deployed on the Cairo-Belgrade-Prague, Cairo-Rome-London, Cairo-Jeddah and Cairo-Khartoum runs. The delivery of the new Comets prompted the airline to shift its Vickers Viscount fleet to regional and domestic lines such as the non-stop link between Cairo and Alexandria. Dakotas were deployed on less important domestic routes including Cairo–Alexandria–Mersa Matruh, Cairo–Assiut–Luxor, Cairo–Luxor–Aswan and Cairo–Port Said–Alexandria routes.[5] Although United Arab Airlines had been established through the merger of Syrian Air and Misrair, many of the UAA aircraft still carried the large logo of Misrair with a smaller logo of UAA. Pleased with the British Comets, two more were ordered in November 1960 and two more in early 1961. Three ex SAS-DC-6s were purchased in April 1961. The Cairo-Lagos run was extended to Accra on 12 June and flights to Moscow commenced on 21 June.

The union between Egypt and Syria ended on 26 September 1961, amid tensions between the leaders of Egypt and Syria. The Syrian Arab Republic was declared in Syria while Egypt chose to continue to carry the title of United Arab Republic until 1971. In parallel to that divorce, Syria withdrew from United Arab Airlines. All the airliners previously owned by Syrian Airways were returned to the Syrian authorities. In Egypt, the flag carrier continued to use the name of United Arab Airlines. A contract with Boeing for the delivery of two Boeing 707-320s with delivery dates between November 1961 and April 1964 fell through when Syria and Egypt ended their union.

Right: This United Arab Airlines Vickers Viscount crashed off the coast of Elba. (Collection of Thijs Postma)

Below: This United Arab Airlines Vickers Viscount was sold to British Eagle upon completion of its service with the Arab carrier. (Ken Fielding/https://www.flickr.com/photos/kenfielding, CC BY-SA 3.0 via Wikimedia Commons)

In 1961, United Arab Airlines obtained three ex-SAS Douglas DC-6B aircraft. (Ralf Manteufel (GFDL) via Wikimedia Commons)

With the introduction of the de Havilland Comet, United Arab Airlines joined the jet age. (EgyptAir)

Above: Passengers join a United Arab Airlines Comet flight. (EgyptAir)

Below left: A January 1961 United Arab Airlines' timetable. (Collection Jozef Mols)

Below right: A July 1962 United Arab Airlines' timetable. (Collection Jozef Mols)

Chapter 5
Russian Planes

Under the presidency of Gamal Abdel Nasser, the Egyptian flag carrier obtained a series of Soviet-made aircraft. This decision was dictated by political factors. In 1950, in order to limit the extent that Arabs and Israelis could engage in an arms race, the three nations that dominated the arms trade in the non-Communist world – the USA, United Kingdom and France – had signed the Tripartite Declaration. By this declaration they had committed themselves to limiting how much arms they could sell in the Near East, and also to ensuring that any arms sales to one side was matched by arms sales of equal quantity and quality to the other side. Nasser who was seen as the leader of the Arab world, wanted to prove he was able to protect Egypt from Israeli agression.[1] After the United Nations criticised a raid by Israel against Egyptian forces in Gaza in 1955, Nasser realised that he could not portray himself as the leader of pan-Arab nationalism if he could not defend his country militarily against Israel. Therefore, he decided to modernise his military and he turned first to the United States for aid.[2] This demand should be seen as a reaction to the French decision to supply Israel with an unlimited quantity of arms in direct violation of the Tripartite Declaration. American President Dwight Eisenhower and Secretary of State John Foster Dulles told Nasser that the USA would supply him with weapons only if they were used for defensive purposes and if he accepted American military personnel for training and supervision. Nasser could not accept these conditions as he advocated a pan-Arab non-alignment. As a result, he turned to the Soviet Union for support. Although Dulles had believed that the USSR would not aid Egypt, he was wrong. The Soviet Union promised Nasser a quantity of arms in exchange for a deferred payment of Egyptian grain and cotton. On 27 September 1955, Nasser announced an arms deal with Czechoslovakia acting as a middleman for the Soviet support. Instead of attacking Nasser for turning to the Soviets, Dulles sought to improve relations with him. In December 1955, the United States and the United Kingdom pledged $56m and $14m respectively towards the construction of the Aswan High Dam. Though the Czech arms deal created an incentive for the US to invest at Aswan, the United Kingdom cited the deal as a reason for repealing its promise of dam funds that had been announced earlier. When Nasser diplomatically recognised China as a communist country, which was in direct conflict with Dulles' policy of containment of communism, the United States also decided to withdraw its offer of funding for the dam. In June 1956, the Soviets offered Nasser a $1.12bn loan at a two per cent interest rate for the construction of the dam. Furthermore, a large number of Egyptian technicians would be trained in the Soviet Union.[3]

Nasser, who had tried to play both sides of the Cold War against each other in favour of the Arab countries and who had tried to remain neutral, was now drawn into the Russian camp. Given these new ties, it was only a matter of time until Soviet aircraft found their way into the fleet of the national airline, which was still known as United Arab Airlines (UAA). However, the UAA fleet, surprisingly, continued to have a British tone well into the 1960s with Vickers Vikings, followed by Viscounts and Comet jets. In the early 1960s, UAA also managed to obtain second-hand Douglas DC-6 aircraft. The first Soviet equipment to enter the fleet was the Antonov 24, of which ten units were delivered from 1965 onwards at a total price of $2.3m. They would replace the Vikings on some domestic routes. In 1965, a domestic subsidiary of UAA was set up – once again called Misrair – to operate all domestic flights, using the Vikings, DC-6s and An-24s. But Misrair would only operate until 1968 when it merged into the parent company after suffering losses. The Antonovs didn't remain in the fleet for long and several of them crashed.

In 1967, UAA had to suspend many of its flights due to the Six-Day War (5–10 June 1967). In mid-May 1967, the Soviet Union issued warnings to Nasser of an impending Israeli attack on Syria. Nasser asked for the immediate withdrawal of the United Nations Emergency Force (UNEF) from the Sinai on 14 May. The same day, he received a warning from King Hussein of Jordan of Israeli-American collusion to drag Egypt into the war. As a result, Egypt dispatched troops to the Sinai. Military leaders in Egypt tried to convince Nasser to start a pre-emptive attack on Israel, which he refused. He thought that the United States would restrain Israel from attacking due to assurances that he received from Washington and Moscow. In turn, he also reassured both powers that Egypt would only act defensively. He also believed that if Israel did attack, Egypt's quantitative advantage in terms of manpower and arms could stave off Israeli forces for at least two weeks, allowing for diplomacy towards a ceasefire. On the morning of 5 June, the Israeli Air Force struck Egyptian air fields, destroying much of the Egyptian Air Force, as well as some UAA aircraft. Israel quickly captured Sinai and the Gaza strip from Egypt, the West Bank from Jordan, and the Golan Heights from Syria. Egypt, Jordan and Syria accepted a UN Security Council ceasefire on 7 June. Egypt's defeat compelled Nasser to resign on 9 June, naming Vice President Zakaria Mohieddin as his successor. Following massive popular demonstrations in his support, Nasser retained power.[4]

Considering the large number of crashes of UAA Antonovs and Comets and the destruction of assets during the war, the airline lacked aircraft. But there were also other reasons. At the time of the fall of the Egyptian monarchy on 18 June 1953, less than half a million Egyptians were considered wealthy; four million people were middle class and 17 million were poor. Fewer than half of primary school-aged children could attend school. Nearly 75 per cent of the population over ten years of age was illiterate. Nasser's policies had changed this. From academic year 1953–54 through 1965–66, overall public school enrollments doubled. Millions of previously poor Egyptians had joined the middle classes through their education and jobs in the public sector. During Nasser's presidency, ordinary citizens enjoyed unprecedented access to housing, education, employment, healthcare, as well as other forms of social welfare.[5] The economy was booming, resulting in higher demand for both domestic and international air travel.

United Arab Airlines was dealing with aircraft manufacturers from both East and West in a quest for more aircraft. A contract worth US$30m, for three Boeing 707-320Cs was signed on 15 June 1966 and included an option for four additional aircraft. These would supplement the remaining Comets on routes across Europe, the Middle East and North Africa. On 1 November, the airline cancelled a stop at Prague on the Cairo-Prague-Moscow service, and in January 1967 UAA started the Cairo-Frankfurt-Copenhagen route. The first Boeing 707 to arrive served the Cairo to London corridor.

Less usual aircraft were also added to the fleet. In August 1968, the airline took delivery of two Ilyushin Il-18s. These aircraft were destined to serve European routes, specifically Eastern Europe. UAA would use a total of four of these aircraft throughout its history, one of which was used on the route to East Berlin. But soon afterwards its acquisition, one of the aircraft (SU-APC) undershot the runway at Aswan and was written off.

On 28 September 1970, Nasser died suddenly. Following the closure of a summit meeting of the Arab League, Nasser suffered a heart attack. He died a few hours later in hospital. His death was received with shock and his funeral procession, through Cairo, was attended by five million mourners. The man who had put Egypt on the modern map was gone.[6]

On 23 May 1971, the acquisition of two Ilyushin IL-62s was announced, scheduled for delivery in June that year. Immediately the aircraft were put into service on European routes, supplementing the Boeing 707s. The IL-62s were introduced on Asian services on 9 July.[7] The airline would use a total of eight of these aircraft. On 10 October 1971, UAA changed its name to EgyptAir after the country changed its name to Arab Republic of Egypt.[8]

A former Misrair Antonov, flying for United Arab Airlines. (Collection Thijs Postma)

In May 1971, the acquisition of Soviet-made Ilyushin IL-62s was announced. (Christian Volpati (GFDL 1.2) via Wikimedia Commons)

Boeing 707s were ordered by United Arab Airlines in 1966 and received the EgyptAir livery after the name change in 1971. (Graham Dinsdale)

Above: Russian Tupolev 154s joined the fleet at about the same time as the 707s arrived. (Alan Bushell)

Right: When Misrair merged with EgyptAir, the new timetables indicated that EgyptAir was a general sales agent for Misrair.

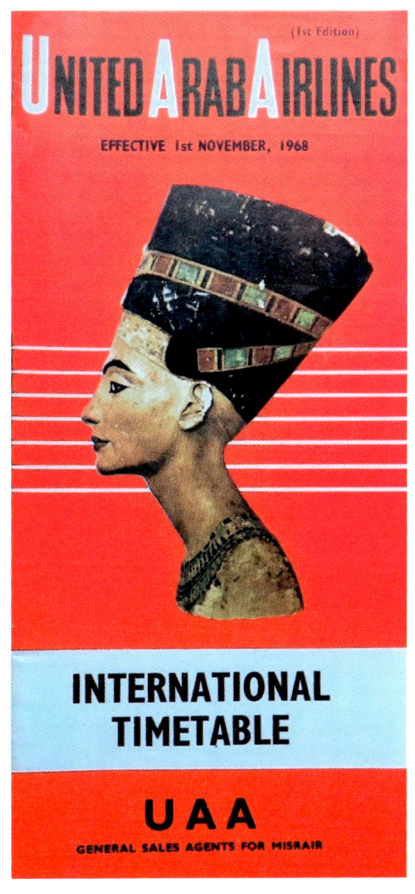

Chapter 6
An All-Boeing Fleet

When Anwar Sadat succeeded Nasser, he adopted more liberal politics and attempted to distance himself from the Soviet Union. Regardless, in 1972, EgyptAir ordered eight Tupolev TU-154s for US$60m with three of them slated for delivery in July 1973, three in November 1973 and two in March 1974. In the meantime, the airline leased two Douglas DC-9-30s from Slovenia's (then part of former Yugoslavia) Inex-Adria, one of which was destroyed during a crash on approach to Aden, Yemen, on 19 March 1972. In June of that year an Ilyushin Il-62 was damaged beyond repair. Four new 707s soon arrived and when also the TU-154s were delivered, the Ilyushin 18s and some IL-62s could be returned to Russia.[1]

The Yom Kippur War – also known as the Ramadan War – began on 6 October 1973 when an Arab coalition launched a surprise attack against Israel on the Jewish holy day of Yom Kippur. Fighting commenced when Egyptian and Syrian forces crossed their corresponding ceasefire lines with Israel and invaded the Sinai Peninsula and the Golan Heights. They initially made gains into Israeli-occupied territory. But after three days of fighting, the Egyptian offensive on the Sinai Peninsula was halted, resulting in a military stalemate on that front. Syrians at the Golan Heights were pushed back to the pre-war ceasefire lines. Israel then launched a four-day-long counter-offensive deep into Syria. On 22 October, an initial ceasefire brokered by the United Nations unravelled, with each side blaming the other for the breach. By 24 October, the Israelis had improved their positions considerably and completed their encirclement of the Egyptian Third Army and Suez City. This development led to dangerously heightened tensions between the United States and the Soviet Union as the Soviets were supporting Arab states and the USA was supporting Israel, the conflict in the Middle East resulted in a conflict between the two sponsors, and a second ceasefire was imposed on 25 October to officially end the war.[2]

The outbreak of the war had forced EgyptAir to suspend its Tokyo service, which was resumed on 15 March 1974 via Bombay, Bangkok and Manila. The same year, the flight to Khartoum was extended to Kinshasa (Democratic Republic of the Congo). When one of the new TU-154s crashed, EgyptAir requested the return of its entire TU-154 fleet to the Soviets, as well as a refund for the price paid for them. The capacity shortage caused by the grounding of the TU-154s was partly alleviated by the lease of other aircraft. The airline had already been looking into the possibility of buying other aircraft and an order for six Douglas DC-9-50s was placed in November. But in January 1975, the Egyptian government cancelled the order for the Douglas jets and moved to Boeing for the provision of new equipment. An agreement with the Soviets was reached for the return of the TU-154s and also the remaining AN-24s were traded back to Aviaexport (the company representing the Soviets) as partial repayment for the loan taken to buy the TU-154s. An order for new Boeing aircraft – including four 727-200s and six 737-200s – was finalised by March 1975. There were plans to trade the first three Boeing 707s in for the new aircraft. Valued at US$60m, the purchase transaction was partly financed by the United Arab Emirates. In May 1975, the order was changed to eight Boeing 737-200s instead of the four ordered earlier slated for April and May 1976. Arrangements were also made to sell the four remaining Comets to raise money to finance the purchase. EgyptAir would then use an all-Boeing fleet.[3]

The Boeing-deal would soon be cause for consternation. An Egyptian parliamentary committee had heard charges by one of its members that officials of EgyptAir had taken commissions on the earlier sale of the Boeing-707 jets. Mohamed Rashwan, the member of parliament, told the Transport Committee he had heard about the commissions, but said he had no concrete proof. The parliamentary committee had also to investigate the US$60m loan arranged by the American investment banking firm of Kidder, Peabody & Company, in 1972, to finance the purchase of four Boeing 707s. Meanwhile, EgyptAir's chairman – Gamal Erfan – had submitted his resignation. The US Securities and Exchange Commission said it had information that Boeing might indeed have made illegal payments to foreign government officials to promote sales.[4] Ezzat Megahed, EgyptAir's financial director, said the company had obtained $53m from Kidder, Peabody in October 1972 and an additional $7m the following year. He stated interest payments accruing on the loans, which would mature in 1984; would total $64.8m or more than the principal capital. A spokesman for Kidder, Peabody replied by stating that the loans in question had been endorsed by the National Bank of Egypt and guaranteed by the Central Bank of Egypt. Kidder, Peabody also stated that payments of the principal and interest on $43m of the loan carried a currency option linked to the exchange rate of the Swiss franc, the West German mark and the Kuwaiti dinar. As a result of the decline in relative value of the American dollar vis-a-vis these currencies, the lenders had exercised this currency option and the debt service requirements had increased proportionately. But that was not the end of the story. A former consultant to EgyptAir was arrested on charges of taking kickbacks for his part in the transaction and he admitted receiving $150,000 for his part in the deal. He also indicated others were implicated in the deal. Two former cabinet ministers were named as suspects. It was, however, clear that no member of President Sadat's Cabinet had been implicated in the 'Boeing affair', nor had any of his close advisers. It became also clear, however, that EgyptAir had paid too much for its Boeings. The airline had paid Boeing $11.5m per plane when the going rate at that time was about $10m. And the money was borrowed from Kidder, Peabody at eight per cent interest when there was evidence that a five per cent loan was available from other sources. The losses from the Boeing deal itself were further aggravated by the wrong use of the aircraft. There were indeed operating losses incurred from using the long-range intercontinental 707s on short hops, for which the cheaper, smaller 727 would have been better suited.[5]

Finally, Mr Shams who had admitted taking bribes was indicted, together with former Deputy Premier and Economy Minister Abdullah Marzeban and former Aviation Minister Ahmed Nouh. They were charged with 'gross negligence' costing the nation US$13.2m. EgyptAir's former chairman, Abdel Hamid Mahmoud and former planning director Ahmed Basraa were charged with 'wilful damage to the public interest'.[6]

But fortunately, there was also some good news. In January 1977, EgyptAir opened the Aviation Services Complex (the biggest and most advanced in the Middle East), meaning the airline could offer services to third parties, thus increasing its income. The step was followed by signing a contract to establish the Cargo Village in October 1978. And in January 1976, the airline had opened the Cairo–Milan route, followed by a new flight to Vienna. To allow further expansion, EgyptAir signed a lease agreement for two Airbus A300B4 aircraft from Germanair and Trans European Airlines in February 1977. On 1 April, services to Abu Dhabi and Karachi were launched. The first leased A300 was used on the Cairo–Karachi route as of 3 June. Later, EgyptAir would change its lease contract into a lease/purchase contract and finally buy the two A300s. During 1979, three more A300B4s were ordered for $115m with a delivery span between September 1980 and September 1981. At the same time, the carrier took options on four more aircraft of the same type. Financing for the three firmly ordered aircraft was partly provided by the Midland Bank and the Dresdner Bank.[7] While waiting for the delivery of the new Airbus aircraft, Egyptair decided to lease two Douglas DC-8-30s for a one-year period.

Above: Waiting for the delivery of the Airbus A300, EgyptAir leased DC-8 aircraft for a one year period. (Collection of Jozef Mols)

Left: A 1977 EgyptAir timetable. (Collection of Jozef Mols)

In 1975, EgyptAir ordered eight Boeing 737-200s. (Alan Bushell)

This Boeing 737-200 was delivered as a government VIP-aircraft in 1976, but joined the EgyptAir fleet in 1986 as SU-GAN. It was transferred, in 1989, to Air Sinai. (Alan Bushell)

EgyptAir leased this Airbus A300 from Belgian carrier TEA. (Bruno Geiger)

Chapter 7
A 'Ghost' Airline

In the early days of 1980, EgyptAir employed 9,610 people, and its fleet consisted of two leased Airbus A300B4s, seven Boeing 707-320Cs, seven Boeing 737-200s and two Beech Barons. There was a major financial reorganisation in November 1980, when ownership of the company was shared by the National Bank of Egypt and the Misr Insurance Company. In 1981, options for two Airbus A300B4-200s were converted into a firm order. This took the count of the A300s pending delivery to four. Another A300B4-200 was ordered in 1982.[1]

The Egypt-Israel peace treaty signed in March 1979 stipulated that there must be active civilian aviation routes between both countries. Earlier, Nefertiti Aviation had performed some charter flights, operated by business jets, on behalf of government officials and business people. To fulfil the treaty, Air Sinai was established in 1982 as a 'paper airline' (meaning a company that has no fleet of its own and rents all its aircraft) for parent company EgyptAir under a wet lease-like agreement.[2] The flights between Israel and Cairo were kept inconspicuous amid lingering hostilities between the nations.[3] Virtually all of the Arab world boycotted Egypt after the peace treaty. This reaction by neighbouring countries, plus the general animosity towards Israel among Egyptian citizens, made Egypt reluctant to fly the Cairo–Tel Aviv route publicly on its national carrier EgyptAir. This reluctance led to the creation of Air Sinai, which allowed Egypt to fulfil the terms of the treaty without directly implicating EgyptAir. Air Sinai used EgyptAir pilots, planes and flight attendants that effectively meant there was no difference between the two airlines, except on paper. The lack of external logos on the planes afforded some privacy to the flight, and many have wondered whether the Egyptian maintained surveillance on travellers between the two countries. The reluctance also meant extreme privacy around Air Sinai's existence. For most of its history, anybody looking for tickets between Cairo and Tel Aviv would find a series of options for airlines offering indirect flights with stops in places such as Amman or Istanbul. But finding a direct flight was more difficult.[4]

Air Sinai had no website, public schedule of flights or mechanism for online bookings. There was no telephone number to call. Though the airline was technically a subsidiary of EgyptAir, its parent pretended there was no connection. The only way to book a ticket through Air Sinai – for those in the know – was to go through a full-service travel agency having found their address through word of mouth. An employee would ask for a scan of the passport page and an international wire transfer to cover the cost of the ticket.[5] The airline only took cash, and often only dollars. For years, passengers would arrive at the Tel Aviv office with envelopes of cash to leave with an old-school yellow airline ticket. Later on, credit cards were accepted. Then, in 2020, flyairsinai.com popped up. Suddenly, everybody had the option to book an Air Sinai flight. Passengers could select any of the daily flights and could pay using a credit card. While one could see this as a sign of increased warmth between Israel and Egypt, the transparency wasn't there. The website described itself as a third-party travel agency only. There was no listed contact information and no social media presence. The site and its developer were based in the United Kingdom. When asked about flyairsinai.com, an Air Sinai employee responsible for booking tickets would deny having any connection to the site, adding an emoji smiley face to the end of the email.[6] The website was short-lived, however, as Air Sinai flights were suspended in 2002, during the Palestinian uprising or intifada, and would resume later but on a smaller scale.[7] In the early days of its existence, Air Sinai used a single unmarked Boeing 737-200 (SU-GAN) on lease from EgyptAir.

A 'Ghost' Airline

By the mid-1980s, a Fokker F27 Friendship was also in service on these routes, as well as on flights from secondary airports in Egypt. During 1982, a Boeing 707-320C was leased and operated on behalf of EgyptAir on flights to Europe, especially twice weekly from Cairo to Copenhagen.[8]

The impact of Air Sinai's operations was minimal on the Egyptian side, as Egyptian tourism to Israel had always been muted. There has always been strong resistance in Egypt against tourism to Israel. Besides, it was very difficult for Egyptians to obtain a visa from the Egyptian government to visit Israel, as well as a visa from the Israeli embassy. The one significant shift came in 2015 when Pope Tawadros II, Pope of the Coptic Church, reversed a ban on visiting Israel, which had been issued by his predecessor in the wake of the 1979 peace treaty. Since then, Egypt's Coptic Christians could visit religious sites in Israel. Though Israeli tourism has decreased, it still exists and Israelis often go incognito about their identity to prevent negative reactions.

While EgyptAir was setting up its 'ghost airline', it also continued to modernise its own fleet. Eight new Airbus A300B4s were introduced during the early 1980s. Four Boeing 767-200ERs (9K-AJA, SU-GAH, SU-GAI, SU-GAJ) were added to the fleet starting in 1984 and the last one would remain in service till 1997. These were followed by three 767-300ERs (SU-GAO, SU-GAP and VH-NOE) in 1989, which remained in service until 2001. SU-GAP, which operated EgyptAir flight 990, crashed into the Atlantic Ocean on a flight between Los Angeles and Cairo with a brief stopover in New York.

In order to cope with the expanding network, EgyptAir was also forced to lease Lockheed L-1011 Tristars in 1989 to 1990 from Canadian airline Air Transat. A first Boeing 747-100 (N480GX) leased from Overseas National Airways entered the fleet in 1983 to 1984, when seven 747-200s arrived (9K-ADA and 9K-ADC from Kuwait Airways, I-DEMV from Alitalia, LX-SAL, N204A, N501Q and SU-GAK). Finally, in 1988, the carrier would receive two Boeing 747-300 Combis, registered SU-GAL and SU-GAM.

Most Air Sinai flights were operated by unmarked EgyptAir aircraft like this Boeing 737-500. (Eassa CC BY-SA 4.0, via Wikimedia Commons)

Some Air Sinai aircraft, like this Boeing 737-200, received a full Air Sinai paint scheme. (G B_NZ CC By-SA 2.0, via Wikimedia Commons)

Air Sinai also operated a Fokker 27 on flights between Israel and regional airports in Egypt. (Collection of Jozef Mols)

Airbus A300B4-200 SU-BCB 'Osiris' was one of the first A300s to be delivered to EgyptAir. (Kambui CC BY 2.0, via Wikimedia Commons)

A new Boeing 767-200 seen in Zürich. (Aero Icarus from Zurich, Switzerland, CC by-SA 2.0, via Wikimedia Commons)

Boeing 767-200 SU-GAJ seen on approach. (Jozef Mols)

One of EgyptAir's newest Boeing 767-200s. (Jozef Mols).

Soon after the arrival of the 767-200s, some 767-300s joined the fleet. This aircraft – operating flight 990 – crashed on 31 October 1999. (Aero Icarus Creative Commons Attribution-Share Alike 2.0 Generic)

An old postcard – issued by the airline – showing a leased Lockheed Tristar. (Collection of Jozef Mols)

After a Boeing 747-100 and a series of 747-200s, EgyptAir obtained this 747-300 in 1988. (contri from Yonezawa, Yamagata, Japan, CC BY-SA 2.0, via Wikimedia Commons)

Boeing 747-300 SU-GAM seen at Munich Airport (Ramin Fischer)

Chapter 8
The Achille Lauro Incident

Hijackings happened often in the Middle East between the 1960s and 1980s. And EgyptAir had a history of such terrorist actions.[1] According to the Aviation Safety Network, the airline had been the victim of no fewer than eight hijackings. In the deadliest, the national flag carrier saw one of its Boeing 737s seized by gunmen said to have links to the Abu Nidal extremist group, in November 1985. They diverted the plane shortly after take-off from Athens, landing in Malta, where a raid by Egyptian commandos resulted in the deaths of 50 passengers and six hijackers. Another hijacking, performed by the United States Air Force resulted in diplomatic tensions between several NATO countries.

Throughout the 1980s, members of the Palestine Liberation Front (PLF) launched attacks on both civilian and military targets in the north of Israel across the Lebanese border. During one such attack on 25 September 1985, they targeted an Israeli yacht in Larnaca, and killed three Israelis. In response, the Israeli Air Force bombed the Palestine Liberation Organisation (PLO) headquarters in Tunis. The headquarters were destroyed and 60 PLO members killed.[2] As is often the case, one retaliation called for another one. Therefore, a new attack on Israel was planned by the PLF.

On 3 October 1985, the cruise ship Achille Lauro, operated by Chandris Line, embarked from Genoa with an itenerary for an eleven-day cruise calling at ports in Alexandria in Egypt and Ashdod in Israel. There were 748 passengers on board, among them four PLF terrorists who planned to sail to Israel in order to attack jewish targets. They travelled with Portuguese, Norwegian and Argentine passports. Because ship hijackings were relatively rare at the time, the cruise line's security was limited to checking passports at Genoa. The terrorists had hidden their weapons in the petrol tank of a car parked in Italy in preparation for boarding the ship. Their smuggled weapons, still with petrol residue on them, emitted a smell that the crew had noticed but not acted upon.

On 7 October, 651 passengers left the ship for a bus tour of the Egyptian pyramids. They were to rendezvous with the ship 14 hours later at Port Said. That day, a cabin steward went to the rooms occupied by the terrorists taking complimentary fruit to leave in the room. On entering he surprised the terrorists while they were cleaning their weapons. Their original plan had been to launch an attack on Ashdod in Israel, but now the plan was put aside as the terrorists panicked and moved to hijack the ship instead. Captain Gerardo de Rosa was ordered by the terrorists to sail 300 miles northeast, to the Syrian port of Tartus.[3] At this point only 97 passengers were on board and became hostages with 450 crew members. Before the hijackers enforced radio silence, the crew sent an SOS that was picked up by a monitoring facility in Sweden. The facility alerted the international community that Palestinians had seized an Italian ship.[4]

Upon learning of the hijacking and that there were Americans on board, members of the Reagan administration in Washington called a meeting of the Terrorist Incident Working Group (including National Security Staff Member Lt Col Oliver North). They recommended that a State Department emergency support team be sent to Rome to assist the embassy there as the vessel was Italian. The Group also recommended that the Pentagon dispatch a team of special operation forces to Europe in case the ship needed to be seized to rescue hostages. Furthermore, the US State Department asked countries along the Mediterranean to deny Achille Lauro access to their ports in order to keep it in international waters. Italian Defence Minister Giovanni Spadolini had the military send 60 paratroopers, four helicopters, and experts on the ship's layout to the British base at Akrotiri in Cyprus. Italian Prime Minister 'Bettino' Craxi looked for a diplomatic solution beginning a dialogue with every country involved. Italy also called on the PLO to publicly declare whether they had any involvement. In response, its Chairman Yasser Arafat denounced the hijacking and offered to assist in negotiating for a peaceful conclusion to the incident. He also sent two men to Egypt to join a negotiating team alongside the Italians and Egyptians. These two men were PLO executive committee member Hani al-Hassan and Abu Abbas.

In the meantime, the terrorists had checked the passports of the passengers and seprated out 20 of them as holders of American or British passports or because they were Jewish. Then, the terrorists broke radio silence and asked Syrian authorities to allow the ship to dock at Tartus. They demanded that a representative from the International Committee of the Red Cross be brought to the ship, along with British and American government representatives. They also asked that the Israeli government be contacted and demanded that 50 Palestinians held in its jails be freed. But Syria, having consulted with the US and Italy, did not respond to any of the demands. In order to make it clear they were serious about their demands, the terrorists threatened to kill hostages if their demands were not met. They selected a Jewish American, Leon Klinghoffer, to be the first victim and shot him.

When Syria did not respond to the demands of the hijackers, the terrorists ordered the ship's captain to sail to Libya. But PLO representative Abbas ordered the hijackers to treat the passengers well and to apologise to them, the crew and the captain. He also ordered the captain to turn back to Port Said where the ship had previously made a tourist stop. In the meantime, the US ambassador to Italy told Prime Minister Craxi that the Americans intended to mount a military assault on the vessel. Craxi, however, protested, stating the ship was Italian and that therefore only Italy should act. Arafat and Abbas communicated to Craxi that the hijackers had promised to release all the passengers unharmed and to drop all demands following pressure from Chairman Yasser Arafat. Egyptian President Hosni Mubarak – who had succeeded Anwar Sadat after his predecessor was murdered in 1981 – pledged to turn over the hijackers to the PLO in Tunis for prosecution.[5] On 9 October, the Achille Lauro anchored off Port Said. The four hijackers left the ship, being taken ashore by the Egyptians in a tugboat. Only much later, the Italian government was informed by the captain of the ship that Klinghofer had been murdered. The American passengers were taken by US military aircraft back to their home country on 12 October 1985.

Ronald Reagan indicated during a press conference that in his opinion, the hijackers should be turned over to a sovereign state that would have jurisdiction and could prosecute them.[6] This way, the problem fell to Egypt's President Hosni Mubarak. The Egyptian government had indeed competing interests that the president was attempting to balance. Mubarak wanted to maintain Egypt's peace treaty with Israel, signed in the margin of the 1978 Camp David Accords. But he also wanted to keep good relations with his fellow Arab states in the Middle East. The Israeli bombing of the PLO office in Tunis had left many innocent Tunisians killed or wounded. Mubarak also wanted to maintain good relations with the US so as not to jeopardise billions of dollars in foreign aid for Egypt. He therefore, tried to get the hijackers out of Egypt as soon as possible. This seemed logical as Egypt had no basis for jurisdiction as the Achille Lauro was of Italian registration, carried no Egyptian passengers, none of the hijackers were Egyptian, and their actions were outside Egyptian territorial limits. The Reagan administration had also sent a series of urgent messages to Cairo, urging the Egyptians to swiftly turn over the hijackers for prosecution to either Italy or the USA. As a result, the hijackers were taken to the airport and left Egypt on board an EgyptAir jet aircraft. Mubarak lied to the press when he said, 'The hijackers have left the country, but I am not going to tell you where they are going.'[7] Learning of the murder of an American citizen, fearing the escape of the hijackers and eager to have a victory over terrorism, Reagan ordered the EgyptAir flight to be forced to land, so that the perpetrators could be brought to justice and he accepted the idea of intercepting the plane.

Israeli diplomats warned Reagan that the jet with the hijackers would fly to Tunisia. Considering ongoing disputes between Egypt and Libya and Chad, it was likely the plane would fly over the Mediterranean Sea, which raised the option of intercepting it with American Navy fighters. Due to anticipated political problems, the idea of forcing the plane to land in either Israel or Cyprus was rejected, and instead, the NATO base in Sigonella (Italy) was chosen. Secretary of Defence Caspar Weinberger, who was not consulted, objected to the idea of intercepting a civilian aircraft when he heard of the plan, but Reagan was not convinced by Weinberger's arguments.

Accompanied by Abu Abbas, Ozzudin Badrakkan (chief of PLF military operations) and several members of Egypt's counterterrorism force, the four hijackers boarded an EgyptAir Boeing 737. The airliner took off from Cairo at 4.15pm destined for Tunis where the PLO headquarters were located. The USS Saratoga, flagship of the Sixth Fleet, had just finished participating in a NATO exercise and was headed for Dubrovnik at that time. It received orders to look for the EgyptAir jet. F-14 Tomcat fighters were launched, together with an E-2D Hawkeye early-warning aircraft. In the meantime, Israeli intelligence had discovered the hijackers were flying on a Boeing 737 with flight number 2843. Soon, the American planes had found the 737. While the Tomcats were following the 737, two US Air Force Lockheed C-141 Starlifter transport aircraft, flying without lights, were carrying special operation troops to Sigonella in order to capture the hijackers should the Navy jets succeed in their mission.

By 5.30pm, the American jets had closed in on the 737, which, unknowingly shadowed by Tomcats, had sought permission to land at Tunis, but the request was refused. A request for permission to land at Athens was also refused. American Hawkeyes and Tomcats started to communicate with the Boeing 737 demanding it divert to Sigonella. When the pilot of the EgyptAir flight refused to comply, the Tomcats received the command 'Lights on, now'. With the illumination of the American aircraft, the Egyptian pilot suddenly realised he was surrounded by warplanes. The Americans ordered him once again to comply or be shot down. Finally, the pilot complied and flew to Sigonella.

Minutes after the 737 touched down, the C-141 cargo planes landed with counter terrorist members of a Sea, Air and Land (SEAL) Team who quickly surrounded the aircraft. The Navy warplanes subsequently closed the airspace overhead for all incoming aircraft. When being informed by radio that the plane was now in the custody of the US military, the pilot told them that an Egyptian ambassador was onboard. The diplomat was allowed to leave the plane and was escorted into the base. The American SEAL team boarded the plane and found the four terrorists. But although they had orders to arrest them, they made no attempt to do so at that time.

Sigonella was an Italian Air Force base in Sicily, which housed a US Navy installation. The American special forces, which had surrounded the 737 soon found themselves surrounded by Italian Air Force soldiers and Carabinieri military police. The Italians insisted that Italy had territorial rights over the base and jurisdiction of the hijackers. A stand-off between the SEAL team and the Italian military began. The Egyptian government, on its side, protested stating the interception of the EgyptAir flight was illegal under international law and therefore should be treated as a hijacking in itself. Not only had the Americans not received consent from the Italians to forcibly land a non-hostile plane flying in compliance with international law at Sigonella, but the American military action was taken solely for American purposes (not those of the NATO alliance).

A stand-off occured when 20 carabinieri and 30 members of the Vigilanza Aeronautica Militare contested for control of the plane with the 80 armed operatives of the US SEAL team. These contesting groups were soon surrounded by 300 additional armed carabinieri who had also blocked the runway with their trucks. They had received authorisation from the Italian President Francesco Cossiga to shoot the Americans if they tried to escape with the hijackers or resist in any other way. During a telephone conversation between Craxi and Reagan, Craxi threatened to attack the American troops at Sigonella. Reagan had to back down. He conceded the Italian claim of jurisdiction over the hijackers and told Craxi that America would seek extradition of the terrorists. After continued talks between Italy and Egypt, the four hijackers were eventually removed from the 737, arrested by the Italian carabinieri and taken to the air base jail. On 11 October, the magistrate in Syracuse announced that his inquiries were complete and EgyptAir 2843 could depart for Rome Ciampino airport. Concerned about the flight, an American pilot boarded a T-39 navy executive jet with other American Special Operations personnel and planned to shadow the 737. But the American jet was not granted clearance from the runway, so it took off using a parallel runway without Italian permission. Italian Starfighter warplanes scrambled and followed the American jet, in turn being followed by American F-14s, which jammed the Italian radar. Once the 737 approached Rome, the formation of American naval fighters turned back with only the T-36 [9] continuing to Ciampino. Once again, the American violation of Italian airspace and landing in a Roman airport without overflight or landing permissions was seen by the Italians as an affront to their laws and safety regulations and negatively influenced diplomatic relations between Italy and the USA for a long time. Diplomatic relations between the USA and Egypt were also negatively impacted as Egypt continued to demand an apology from the US for the hijacking of a civilian airliner and forcing the aircraft off course.

After long discussions within the Italian government, Italy decided Abu Abbas could leave Italy as there was insufficient evidence to link him to the hijacking of the Achille Lauro. Together with Badrakkan and the Egyptian diplomat Zeid Imad Hamed, they flew from Ciampino to Fiumicino airport. Once in Rome's principal airport, they crossed the ramp – escorted by Italian security forces – and embarked on a Yugoslav aircraft, flying to Belgrade. On 10 July 1986, an Italian court ruled the Palestinians guilty of 'carrying out a kidnap with terrorist intent, leading to the death of a hostage'. The court did not refer to the hijackers as terrorists, rather calling them 'soldiers fighting for their ideals'. Three of the hijackers were sentenced to prison terms ranging from 15 to 30 years. Youssef Majed Mosqi, the hijacker who had shot Klinghofer, received one of the longest sentences of the group. The court cited, however, the conditions of his childhood, growing up surrounded by violence in a Palestinian refuge camp as a mitigating circumstance.[8]

EgyptAir, although not directly involved in the Achille Lauro hijacking, came into the spotlight because it transported the hijackers and its 737 was subsequently hijacked by American war planes and consequently received a lot of negative publicity. The United States never apologised for hijacking one of EgyptAir's planes.

Chapter 9
Expansion

During the 1980s and 1990s, EgyptAir grew from a fleet of 14 aircraft to one of 40 aircraft, each with an average age of five and a half years.[1] Initially, Mohamed Fahim Rayan who had become president of the carrier, had ordered a total of eight Airbus A300-B4 aircraft to serve the European and Middle Eastern markets. Later on, he added Boeing 767s. Starting in 1991, EgyptAir took delivery of not less than 12 Airbus A320-200 jets, the last of which would remain in service until 2020. In 1995, the carrier had added three Airbus A340-200s to its fleet, which would remain in service until 1997. In August 1995, EgyptAir ordered three Boeing 777-200ERs to be handed over in 1997. The carrier had opted for a tri-class 308 passenger seating arrangement.[2] Both the Airbus and Boeing aircraft had to cover the requirements of the North American and Japanese markets with destinations to New York, Los Angeles and Tokyo and replaced the A300s and Boeing 767s. Also in 1997, five new Boeing 737-500s were added to serve the tourist attractions in Egypt.

When looking for a livery, EgyptAir had turned to Egypt's history. When the airline started operations in the 1930s, it simply used the country's flag on its aircraft and promotional material. This flag was orginally composed of the red, white and black horizontal stripes of the Arab Liberation Flag from the 1950s, but was modified by adding two green stars in the center to represent Syria and Egypt once United Arab Airlines had been formed as a joint flag-carrier for both countries. However, the United Arab Republic, which joined Syria and Egypt, had collapsed in the 1960s and United Arab Airlines changed its name to EgyptAir. As a newly rebranded carrier EgyptAir selected the sky god Horus as its motif. Horus, often depicted as a falcon or just the Eye of Horus, would often be painted on sea vessels in the hope of safe travels during the time of the ancient Egyptian empire. Horus would make his first appearance on an EgyptAir aircraft in the 1970s and would be painted with a red head and blue feathers on a gold backdrop. The Horus logo would also appear on engine casings. The airline's livery would keep the warm colour theme, using red and gold 'cheat lines' on early liveries and branding. This livery remained untouched for almost 25 years. In the 1990s, however, a colour change was made and blue became the dominant colour for the airline. Horus would remain unchanged in structure, but the blue feathers would be replaced with gold and the gold circle that surrounded him would be exchanged for an all-blue tail. The sky god would also hold its position on the engine covers, but like the tail, be surrounded by the colour blue. As part of the new logo, the airline would alter its branding to show the entire EgyptAir aircraft tail instead of just the Egyptian god on its marketing material. The carrier also introduced an inflight magazine under the name Horus to be read in English and Arabic. Soon, older aircraft in the fleet were repainted with the new livery while new entries in the fleet received the new colours before delivery.[3]

Disaster

Unfortunately, there was no good news for EgyptAir. The Achille Lauro incident had catapulted the airline to the front pages of the news all over the world. In the West, the episode generated negative sentiment towards the airline, whereas in the Middle East, EgyptAir was praised for its help in solving the crisis. A few years later, on 31 October 1999, destiny called again. EgyptAir 990 was a regularly scheduled flight from Los Angeles to Cairo with a stop at John F. Kennedy International Airport in New York. On this day, the Boeing 767 crashed into the Atlantic Ocean about 100km (60 miles) south of Nantucket Island in Massachusetts, killing all 217 passengers and crew on board.[4] Since the crash occured in international waters, it was investigated by the Ministry of Civil Aviation's Egyptian Civil Aviation Agency (ECAA) and the National Transportation Safety Board (NTSB). As the ECAA lacked the resources of the NTSB, the Egyptian government asked the American government to have the NTSB handle the investigation. Two weeks after the crash, the NTSB proposed handing over the investigation to the Federal Bureau of Investigation (FBI) as the evidence they had collected suggested that a criminal act had taken place and that the crash was intentional rather than accidental. The Egyptians refused the proposal and so, the NTSB was forced to continue the investigation alone. According to the NTSB evidence, the accident was caused due to the aircraft's departure from normal cruise flight as 'result of the relief first officer's flight control inputs'. The cockpit crew had consisted of 57-year old Captain Ahmed El-Habashi, and 36-year old First Officer Adel Anwar who switched duty with another co-pilot so he could return home in time for his wedding. The relief crew consisted of 52-year old Captain Raouf Nouredin, 59-year old First Officer Gameel Al-Batouti, and the airline's Boeing 767 chief pilot Hatem Rushdy. As the flight time was ten hours, the flight required two complete flight crews. EgyptAir designated one crew as the 'active crew' and the other as the 'cruise crew' or 'relief crew'. Usually, the active crew made the take-off and would fly the first four to five hours of flight. The cruise crew would then assume control until about one or two hours before landing, when the active crew returned to the cockpit. While on this flight, the cruise crew was intended to take over far into the flight, relief officer Al-Batouti entered the cockpit and recommended that he relieve the command first officer 20 minutes after take-off. Command first officer Anwar first protested but eventually relented. Shortly afterwards, captain El-Habashi left the cockpit to go to the lavatory. During that time, relief first officer Al-Batouti was alone in the cockpit. At 1.48.39, he began to exclaim 'I rely on God' and at 1.49.45 disengaged the autopilot. The autopilot disengagement warning was not heard on the Cockpit Voice Recorder (CVR) indicating the autopilot was disengaged manually. At 1.49.53, the throttles of both engines were moved to idle and only one second later the aircraft entered an increasingly steep dive, resulting in weightlessness (zero gravity) throughout the cabin. Nevertheless, the captain managed to regain the cockpit. At that time, the speed of the aircraft was dangerously close to the sound barrier, exceeding the design limits. At 1.50.19, the flight reached its maximum rate of descent of 12,000m (39,000ft) per minute. Between 1.50.20 and 1.50.23 the captain began to pull back on his control column while relief first officer Al-Batouti moved both engines' start levers from the 'run' to the 'cut-off' position, shutting off fuel flow to the engines. The captain reacted by pushing them back to their maximum position without result. The captain then deployed the speedbrakes, which slowed the aircraft's dive, bringing it back to a safer speed. Without fuel, both engines ran down to a stop, causing the aircraft to loose all electrical power, including to both flight recorders and the aircraft's transponder. The last secondary radar return from the flight was received at 1.50.34, the Flight Data Recorder stopped recording at 1.50.36 and the CVR stopped at 1.50.38.[5] As the recorders had stopped working, only radar data can provide information about what happened next. At approximately 1.50.38, the aircraft entered a steep climb, presumably due to the abrupt manoeuvres made by the captain to recover from the dive. At 1.51.15, the aircraft entered another steep dive. At some point during the final descent, the left engine and some other small pieces of debris separated from the aircraft due to extreme structural stresses.[6]

Examination of the recorders revealed that the captain had gone to the lavatory, followed some 30 seconds later by the first officer saying 'Tawkalt al Allah' meaning 'I put my trust in God'. Three seconds later the throttles were reduced to idle and both elevators were moved three degrees nose down. When the captain returned, he asked, 'What's happening?' The flight data recorder then revealed that the elevators moved into a split condition with the left elevator up and the right elevator down. This condition can be expected to result when the two control columns are subjected to at least 50lb of opposing force. The captain was heard asking, 'What is this? Did you shut down the engines?' Then the captain is heard repeatedly saying, 'pull with me', but the FDR indicated that the elevator surfaces remained in a split condition.[7]

Considering all these factors, the NTSB concluded that the relief first officer Al-Batouti had deliberately stopped the engines of the aircraft and then initiated a steep dive. When the captain returned to the cockpit, he had tried to save the aircraft, but was deliberately opposed by the first officer. Therefore, it became clear the crash was a deliberate suicide attempt by the first officer. EgyptAir did not accept this conclusion and explained the crash as the result of 'technical problems'. All the scenarios it suggested were tested in flight simulators, but none were logical or even possible.

In February 2000, EgyptAir 767 captain Hamdi Hanafi Taha sought political asylum in London. In a statement to the authorities, he attested that first officer Al-Batouti had intentionally crashed the plane as revenge on an airline executive, who had recently demoted Al-Batouti and was on board the doomed flight. EgyptAir officials immediately dismissed Taha's claims, but American investigators confirmed key aspects of Taha's information. The NTSB did not issue an official statement about Al-Batouti's motive. EgyptAir terminated Taha's employment and his application for British asylum was declined.[8]

Airbus A300-600R SU-GAU joined the fleet in the second half of 1991. (Jozef Mols)

This Airbus A300B4 was leased out by EgyptAir to Kuwait Airways and Air Alfa before joining the EgyptAir Cargo fleet. This explains the non-standard livery. (Jozef Mols)

Above: In 1991, EgyptAir received new Boeing 737-500s, here seen in the old livery. (Aero Icarus from Zürich, Switzerland, via Wikimedia Commons)

Left: This Boeing 747-300 received the new livery. (contri from Yonezawa-Shi, Yamagata, Japan, CC BY-SA 2.0, via Wikimedia Commons)

Below: In 1991, EgyptAir received its first Airbus A320-200s. (Jozef Mols)

One of EgyptAir's new Airbus A320-200s. (Jozef Mols)

An A320 showing the new livery of EgyptAir. (Jozef Mols)

Above: The new Airbus A340 was delivered with the new livery. (Jozef Mols)

Left: Together with the A340, EgyptAir also added the Boeing 777 to its fleet. (Rob Hodgkins, CC BY-SA 2.0, via Wikimedia Commons)

An EgyptAir Boeing 777-200ER seen at Narita Airport in Japan. (Ken Fielding/https://www.flickr.com/photos/kenfielding, CC BY-SA 3.0, via Wikimedia Commons)

Chapter 10
Restructuring

During its history, EgyptAir had not limited its activities to scheduled and charter flights. The carrier had provided a whole series of services, directly or indirectly linked to the operations of airlines and airports. It had set up its own maintenance facilities, a ground service company, an in-flight service company and had also operated cargo flights. In July 2002, the company was restructured into a holding company with subsidiaries. These included EgyptAir Maintenance and Engineering Company, EgyptAir Ground Services Company, EgyptAir Cargo Company, EgyptAir Inflight Services Company, EgyptAir Tourism and Duty Free Shops Company, and EgyptAir Medical Services Company. Later, in 2006, EgyptAir Supplementary Industries Company was added.[1]

EgyptAir Inflight Services would provide services for the entire fleet of EgyptAir, and also for other carriers. The company handles on-board sales, manufactures dry ice, manages cafeterias and restaurants, and provides laundry services as well as outside catering. EgyptAir Medical Services initially offered its services only to EgyptAir employees and their families. Later on, the services were extended to cover all civil aviation field workers. In recent years, medical services to the public, healthcare medical insurance companies and medical programmes for tourists were added. EgyptAir Supplementary Industries – which was added in 2006 – manufactures all non-structural items and all other plastic items used for in-flight catering. It also produces printed materials for administrative activities. It also manufacturers uniforms.

The restructuring marked the end of a 21-year period in which the airline was headed by Mohamed Fathim Rayan, who was criticised for his perceived resistance to liberalisation of the aviation sector, and in particular his refusal to allow scheduled flights to serve airports near tourist resorts. The new holding would, in the future, be headed by Abdel Fattah Kato.[2] The government appeared to have forgotten that Rayan fulfilled his task under very difficult circumstances, with tensions and wars between Arab countries and Israel, which had put pressure on Egypt's tourism industry resulting in decreasing passenger numbers. The terrorist attacks in New York on 9/11 also resulted in a worldwide decrease in air travel. EgyptAir had seen its passenger traffic drop 40 per cent.[3]

Shorouk Air

Shorouk Air, the carrier that had been set up in September 1992 as a joint venture between EgyptAir and Kuwait Airways had gone bankrupt. Its intention was to offer charter flights from Western Europe to Egypt, as well as regular scheduled flights to destinations in the Middle East. Originally, it was planned to start with a leased DC-8-73 from investment group Guinness Peat Group, although eventually an Airbus A320 was selected. Due to poor results, an order for some Boeing 757s was cancelled and the two A320s in the fleet had been leased out to Oasis Airlines (SU-RAA) and Trans Alsace (SU-RAB) in the spring of 1994. When the aircraft returned from Oasis, it was leased out to Onur Air in Turkey. The second A320 was leased out to Albanian Airlines. In autumn 1996, Shorouk planned to obtain a third A320 but instead leased a similar aircraft from Onur Air.

The Luxor massacre on 17 November 1997 during which 58 tourists were killed, resulted in a deep crisis for the Egyptian tourism industry.

In October 1999, Shorouk leased an A320 (EI-TLP) from TransAer in Ireland, and in November, another aircraft from Airfinance, but in July 2003, the airline had ceased its operations due to a drop in passenger numbers. By that time, foreign charter companies had started operating to Egypt and even some low-cost carriers had entered the market. Shorouk could not compete with them.

The new president of the group, Abdel Fattah Kato, would not be able to turn the tide immediately. The company's losses exceeded US$300m (£244m) in the financial year 2002–03.[4] The restructuring coincided with the establishment of the Egyptian Ministry of Civil Aviation and the government's ambitious strategy to modernise and upgrade its airports and airline. EgyptAir was given the right to operate without interference from the government and the duty to do so without any financial backing.[5]

A cost-cutting programme was devised, which included restructuring the company's fleet. A deal to buy five new Airbus A318s and two A340-600s was cancelled.[6] To cut back on maintenance costs, the airline also planned to halve the number of aircraft types in its fleet to five. EgyptAir prepared to put its Boeing 777 and 747 jets up for sale by the end of 2003. At the same time it placed an order for seven A330-200s, powered by Rolls-Royce Trent 700 engines.[7] Deliveries were due to commence in June 2004. The new Airbus aircraft were intended to replace the ageing A300-600Rs. For its short-haul operations, the airline also obtained some ATR-42-500s in 2003 on a one-year lease.

To replace tourist flights, previously organised by Shorouk Air, EgyptAir started negotiations to acquire a 40 per cent stake in a new private airline, Air Cairo. Bank of Egypt and Banque du Caire each had a 20 per cent stake in the new company. Operations were due to start in September, concentrating on charter flights to Egypt's main tourist resorts.[8]

Shorouk Air was a joint venture between EgyptAir and Kuwait Airways and ceased operations in 2003. (Jozef Mols)

The EgyptAir In-flight services building. (Faris knight, CC BY-SA 3.0, via Wikimedia Commons)

EgyptAir Ground Services Company is active on all Egyptian airports. (David Adel and Heba Khalil 2 CC0 1.0, via Wikimedia Commons)

Chapter 11

Air Cairo

Setting up Air Cairo was a major step for EgyptAir, which anticipated countering competition from foreign and Egyptian carriers, which had entered the market. Actually, Air Cairo had already been incorporated in 1997 by Ibrahim Kamil. At first the airline only operated cargo flights, using two Tupolev 204s, but soon a contract was signed for the wet-lease of one of its aircraft to TNT Express. Air Cairo also operated ad-hoc charter flights for tour operators. When Shorouk Air, which was 51 per cent owned by EgyptAir, ceased operations in 2003, there was room for new capacity in the Egyptian IT-charter market. Therefore, Kamil restructured his company. EgyptAir (40 per cent) and Banque du Caire (20 per cent) became the new shareholders in his airline. The new company was re-incorporated in August 2003 with an initial capital of 100m Egyptian pounds (approx £3.363m). The name of the original Air Cairo was used for the new airline, whereas the 'old' Air Cairo was renamed Cairo Aviation. The new airline had headquarters at Cairo International Airport and started operating charter flights between Europe and Egypt on behalf of tour operators. These flights took off from Cairo, but also from Sharm El Sheikh International Airport and Hurghada International Airport. Besides, Air Cairo started operating scheduled flights to the Middle East and Europe. Shortly after its incorporation, Kamil sold his shares in the new airline. From that date onwards, EgyptAir would own 60 per cent, with National Bank of Egypt and Bank Misr each holding 20 per cent. The first aircraft – an Airbus A321-200 – joined the fleet in October 2003, followed by a second one in August 2004 and an Airbus A320-200 in November 2005.[1]

EgyptAir's participation in Air Cairo should be seen against the background of the liberalisation of Egyptian aviation. Several investors (often with Saudi backing) had set up new ventures and competed with EgyptAir's regular scheduled flights. AMC Airlines is probably the best known of these new ventures. The company was established in 1988, after the Egyptian government approved the foundation of Aircraft Maintenance in Cairo. At that time, Elsayed Saber and his family launched AMC Aviation after obtaining a licence to operate worldwide charter flights. The airline started operating from Cairo International Airport and had hubs in Hurghada International Airport, Sharm el-Sheikh International Airport and Luxor International Airport. Although the airline was authorised to operate worldwide flights, most of its activities were centred around charter flights to Europe and scheduled domestic flights.[2] The airline started its operations with a single Boeing 737-200 in 1993 (five years after the company was established), followed by a 737-400 in 1996 and a McDonnell Douglas MD-90 in 1998. In 2004, the airline was renamed AMC Airlines.

In August 1995, Air Memphis was established as a charter airline based in Cairo. Two years later, Lotus Air was set up by the Al-Fawares Holding Company. The airline started its operations in 1998 from its main base at Cairo International Airport with hubs at Sharm el-Sheikh International Airport, Hurghada International Airport and Luxor International Airport. Besides offering charter flights, the company also provided aircraft, crew, maintenance and insurance (ACMI) flights, damp leases (lease of aircraft without crew), technical services, ground handling and crew training. It was the first airline in Egypt to receive EASA standards maintenance certification and IATA Operational Safety Audit (IOSA) certification. The airline concentrated its fleet around the Airbus A320 family with the A320, A321 and A319 in its fleet.[3] In 1998, Midwest Airlines was founded with an intial fleet of two Airbus A310-300s. From its beginning, the airline offered charter services from Egyptian holiday resorts to Europe and the Middle East on behalf of local and international tour operators. Midwest Airlines ceased its operations in 2006.[4]

In 1998, the Dutch airline Jet Link Holland set up an Egyptian branch by establishing Tristar Air together with the Messch family. The new carrier started operating cargo flights between Egypt and the Netherlands in direct competition with EgyptAir's cargo branch – but after the loss of its only aircraft in 2015, it ceased operations.[5] Other newcomers on the Egyptian aviation scene were Pharaoh Airlines (1998), and Raslan Air Services (1996). Raslan only operated domestic flights and charter flights with its Saab 340.

Obviously, the creation of Air Cairo was not enough to counter the increasing competition. Since restructuring the company in 2002, EgyptAir had pursued a three-pronged strategy based on safety, customer orientation and effective competition. To realise this strategy the company focused on building an integrated human, information and physical infrastructure to form a platfom for growth. It invested heavily in the information infrastructure and implemented the Amadeus reservation system, e-ticketing, as well as many other automated systems in maintenance, cargo and other applications including inventory management, multi-channel sales and reservations plus distribution and departure control services. To improve its competitive stance in its markets, one of its major strategic moves has been to actively pursue a variety of long-term alliances, including relationships with Star Alliance member airlines such as Lufthansa, Singapore Airlines, Austrian Airlines, Thai Airways International, Swiss International Airlines, South African Airways, Turkish Airlines and BMI. With Lufthansa, cooperation was also started in the fields of cargo, maintenance and in-flight services.[6] On 16 October 2007, the Chief Executive Board of the Star Alliance voted to accept EgyptAir as a future member. In July 2008, the airline effectively joined the alliance to become the only member based in North Africa and the Middle East. Being a member of the Star Alliance gave more advantages to customers of the airline as the alliance's network covered 1,290 destinations in 189 countries around the world, at that time. EgyptAir chief executive Atef Abdel Hamid outlined plans to turn Cairo into a hub for North Africa and the Middle East, aided by the expansion of Cairo's airport. A new terminal was planned to open in 2008 and would become a dedicated Star Alliance terminal.[7] Egypt has indeed a strategic location which offers a good link between Africa, the Middle East and Europe to the rest of the world. For the first time, rumours were heard about a possible offering of 20 per cent of EgyptAir's shares to the public. When the airline joined the Star Alliance however, the plan was cancelled.[8]

In the meantime, EgyptAir Maintenance and Engineering had also acquired the European Aviation Safety Agency (EASA) part 145s to perform maintenance on Airbus aircraft. This approval was later further expanded to include Boeing types. By the end of 2007, EgyptAir Maintenance and Engineering fulfilled the requirement to be a certified organization according to ISO 9001, 2000, ISO 17025 was also granted for the callibration lab. A new engine overhaul workshop was opened in 2008, for which EASA approval was obtained in March 2008.

The airline also had ordered nine Boeing 737-800s for delivery between 2006 and 2009. The order was worth US$864m (£716m) at list price. Eight of the aircraft would be financed by lessor Dubai Aerospace Enterprise.

Above: An Air Cairo Airbus A320 seen at Dusseldorf Airport. (Ken Fielding/https://www.flickr.com/photos/kenfielding, CC BY-SA 3.0, via Wikimedia Commons)

Left: An Air Cairo Airbus A 321. (Jozef Mols)

Below: AMC became one of EgyptAir's main competitors when it launched operations with this Boeing 737-200. (Jozef Mols)

Above: AMC – EgyptAir's competitor – leased this McDonnell Douglas MD90-30 from Uni Air in Taiwan. (Jozef Mols)

Right: This Airbus A 300 was used by AMC between 1998 and 2004. (Jozef Mols)

Below: Air Memphis started operations in 1995. (Björn Strey BY-SA 2.0 via Wikimedia Commons)

Lotus Air was set up in 1997 and operated Airbus A320s. (Jozef Mols)

Midwest Airlines used the Airbus A310. (Aero Icarus from Zürich, Switzerland, CC BY-SA 2.0 via Wikimedia Commons)

When EgyptAir joined the Star Alliance, some of its aircraft, like this 777, received a special paint scheme, depicting the alliance's logo. (John Taggart from Sunbury on Thames, Middlesex, CC BYU-SA 2.0, via Wikimedia Commons)

Also this Boeing 737-800, delivered in 2008, received the Star Alliance logo. (Star Alliance)

Chapter 12
EgyptAir Express

While Air Cairo had been set up to counter competition from charter- and low-cost airlines that had flooded the Egyptian market, EgyptAir decided, in 2006, to set up one more subsidiary. In May 2006, EgyptAir Express was launched as a domestic feeder carrier for EgyptAir. The new airline started operations with a fleet of Embraer E-170LR jets, leased from its parent company. The airline would receive a total of 12 of these jets, the last of which was delivered in 2009. Several airports in Egypt, including Sharm el Sheikh, Hurghada, Luxor, Aswan, Marsa Alam, Abu Simbel and Alexandria were then linked with Cairo International Airport. At the same time, the airline considered starting flights from Sharm el Sheikh to regional destinations including Jeddah and Amman, which were expected to be excellent markets during the summer season. In its first year of operation, the airline transported 909,149 passengers, resulting in a load factor of 80 per cent. EgyptAir Express indicated net profits after taxes of EGP 6.6m. (£221,000).[1] A year later, the airline had obtained 46 per cent of the market share and had carried 1,130,040 passengers, resulting in a net profit of EGP15m.(£502,000).[2] In 2009, a total of 1,500,000 passengers flew EgyptAir Express on 26,000 flights,. The load factor on these flights reached 77 per cent and EgyptAir Express became the dominant airline in the domestic market with a 52 per cent market share.[3]

Parent company EgyptAir was also doing well. The airline had made a profit of EGP161,173,885 (£5.4m) in 2007. The total number of passengers reached 5,716,528 (up from 4,974,808 one year earlier). Flights to other destinations in the Middle East remained the main business of the airline, transporting 1.7 million passengers. Europe came second with a total number of one million tickets sold. Its flights to Asian destinations reported 45 per cent growth largely due to increasing direct flights to Bangkok, as well as re-opening the route to Beijing. In this time EgyptAir improved its flight punctuality from 79.1 per cent in 2002 to 87.5 per cent in 2007.[4]

After setting up Air Cairo and EgyptAir Express, EgyptAir partnered with the Egyptian Ministry of Civil Aviation and the Egyptian Holding Company for Airports & Navigation to form a new corporate airline, Smart Aviation Company, based at Cairo Airport.[5] The new company launched its operations during the second quarter of 2007 and became the first corporate jet operator in the country. In 2009, it would expand its business portfolio to cover medical evacuation in the form of air ambulance operations.

While EgyptAir was rapidly expanding, the airline updated its logo. In 2008, the Horus logo was altered when the airline announced what would become its latest rebranding. The Horus design would be streamlined by removing the facial features and keeping the eye and feathers. For the first time, Horus would also drop the red and gold colours from his design, being left with a new design that featured multiple shades of blue. That year – 2008 – EgyptAir transported 6.7m passengers, but the load factor had dropped to 67 per cent, due to the increased flight frequencies and the opening of new routes. Nevertheless, profits reached EGP 232m (£7.7m).

In 2009, EgyptAir's operations at the Cairo International Airport (where it held 61 per cent of the airport's departure slots) were notably overhauled due to the inauguration of the new terminal 3 in April 2009. The airline transferred all its operations (international and domestic) to the new terminal that had more than doubled the airport's capacity. Under the Star Alliance 'Move Under One Roof' concept, all Star Alliance airlines serving Cairo had moved to this Terminal 3. It was planned to also overhaul operations at the Alexandria base by transferring operations from the older facilities at Alexandria International Airport to the new airport in Borg El Arab. And at the same time, it was rumoured EgyptAir was evaluating the possibility of setting up a low-cost subsidiary for its Alexandria operations to address the growth of LCC's in that city.[6]

During the 2009–10 Paris Airshow, the airline announced a new venture with US lessor Aviation Capital Group and other Egyptian private and public shareholders to establish a leasing joint venture, focusing on the Middle East and Northern African region. The new joint venture – named Civil Aviation Finance and Operating Leases or CIAF Leasing – would initially focus on narrowbody aircraft[7], as well as on airport equipment. In the meantime, EgyptAir Maintenance & Engineering had been nominated 'The Best Airline Third Party MRO' in the yearly Aviation Industry Awards, alongside AFI/KLM E&M and Lufthansa Technik. EgyptAir's passenger count had increased to 7.3 million by 2010 with a load factor of 72 per cent. But net profits had dropped to EGP 130m (£4.4m). EgyptAir Express had increased its number of routes to 20 (from 11 at the date of its incorporation) by including destinations in Greece, Lebanon and Saudi Arabia.

Unfortunately, for EgyptAir, the tide turned in 2010 when the Arab Revolution started. The catalyst was the self-immolation of Tunisian Mohamed Bouazizi. His death, on 4 January 2011, sparked revolution that spread around the Arab world. Protests in Egypt began on 25 January 2011 and went on for 18 days. Thousands of people mobilised in Egypt's major cities, President Hosni Mubarak dismissed his government. On 10 February Mubarak ceded all presidential power to Vice President Omar Suleiman., Suleiman announced that Mubarak had resigned and transferred power to the Armed Forces of Egypt.

Tourists cancelled their holiday plans to Arab countries amid safety concerns. By the end of the year, EgyptAir announced a loss of EGP 2.2m. (£73,000).[8]

This Boeing 737-500 received the new EgyptAir paint scheme introduced in 2008. (Collection of Jozef Mols)

This Airbus A320-200 – seen at Brussels Airport – was painted with the new EgyptAir paint scheme. (Lentokonefani, CC BY-SA 4.0, via Wikimedia Commons)

This Boeing 737-800 was delivered in 2009. (Alan Bushell)

EgyptAir Express

This Airbus A321 was repainted with the new colour scheme. (Collection Jozef Mols).

EgyptAir's cargo fleet received the new colour scheme, seen here on an Airbus A300-600 (Alec Wilson from Khon Kaen, Thailand, CC BY-SA 2.0, via Wikimedia Commons)

This Embraer ERJ-170LR was one of the first aircraft in the EgyptAir Express Fleet. (Raymond Zamitt)

The Smart Aviation Company was set up as a joint-venture between EgyptAir and several governmental investors and started to offer corporate aviation services. (Smart Aviation Company)

During the Arab Revolution, passengers fleeing the violence, overcrowded the airport in Cairo.
(Floris Van Cauwelaert CC BY-SA 2.0, via Wikimedia Commons)

Chapter 13
Crisis

In February 2011, passenger numbers had fallen by 65.5 per cent across Egypt's airports.[1] Egypt's civil aviation minister Wael El Maadawi said the airline lost an estimated EGP 1.3bn or around £114m over the 2012/13 fiscal year, mainly due to an increase in fuel prices, the devaluation of the Egyptian currency and continuous strikes within the company. Losses for 2011/12 were apparently around double the 2012/2013 figures, although it is difficult to obtain exact figures.[2] The impact of the revolution was not mentioned but it had undermined EgyptAir's expansion plans.

In 2011, EgyptAir had started operating non-stop flights to Guangzhou, besides a new frequency to Juba (Southern Sudan). Also the frequencies to Johannesburg and Beijing had been increased. And in the beginning of November 2011, EgyptAir had restored its operation to Benghazi in Libya, followed by direct flights to Tripoli.

A few years earlier, the airline had received the first of three Airbus A340-200s alongside another similar aircraft, leased from Gulf Air. These aircraft had been ordered along with three General Electric GE90-powered Boeing 777s to supplement the long-haul fleet and replace the airline's fleet of Airbus A300B4s and Boeing 767-200s.[3] The new Airbus jets would be used on long-distance flights to Japan, Australia and Singapore.[4] Due to the Arab Revolution, the airline however had to ground the new aircraft as many routes were discontinued due to lack of passengers. One A340-200 – the only one which remained in the fleet at that time – would be reactivated only in 2014.[5] In August 2010, the airline had also received the first Airbus A330-300[6], but once again, the new jets would fly a reduced programme. As a result of the slump in traffic and revenues EgyptAir started discussions with Airbus with a view to deferring some of its A330-300 deliveries so that it could stabilise its operations. At that time, the airline had also received the fifth of six Boeing 777-300Ers, which were intended to open routes to Toronto and Washington, but were now postponed.[7]

Besides the direct impact of the revolution on EgyptAir's operations and revenue, other factors were also cause for concern. A group of female flight attendants had been calling for their right to wear the hijab. At the same time, a group of male flight attendants demanded the right to grow beards. This move came in the aftermath of the revolution, the election of former Muslim Brotherhood member Mohamed Morsy as president and calls to apply Sharia law in a new constitution.

In November 2012, EgyptAir approved the hijab pending distribution of the company's new uniform.[8] Some marketeers feared the move might scare away tourists. To complete the negative picture, EgyptAir's pilots staged a 10-hour sit-in at Cairo's international airport in June 2013 to demand management changes and bonus payments, delaying 22 flights. Around the same time, Egypt's civil aviation minister said the national airline had lost more than EGP 7bn (£831m) since the 2011 uprising.[9]

Nile Air

The Arab Spring was not the only factor affecting EgyptAir's business. A new wave of entrants to the market had increased competition and eroded ticket prices and profit margins. Nile Air had been established in 2006 and intended to operate scheduled services to destinations in Egypt, the Middle East, the Persian Gulf, Southern Europe, Asia and Africa.

Nile Air had received its AOC (Air Operators Certificate) in November 2009, which permitted the company to launch operations using a fleet of Airbus A320-200s and Airbus A321-200s. Nile Air had launched operations in August 2010, operating a short-term wet-lease contract with Libyan Arab Airlines before starting scheduled services from Egypt to Saudi Arabia in March 2011. In January 2011, the airline had become the first private Egyptian carrier to publish its schedule and flight availability on the Global Distribution System (GDS) so that it was covered on all three GDS systems (Amadeus, Sabre Corporation and Travelport). In 2013, Nile Air joined the Arab Air Carriers Organization and the African Airlines Association.[10]

Nesma Airlines

Nesma Airlines was established in 2007. The airline operated its first commercial flight on 18 July 2010 from Hurghada to Ljubljana. It also started operating charter flights linking Egypt, Europe (UK, Italy, Spain, Poland, France), and the Middle East (Saudi Arabia). The airline had started operating scheduled flights to Saudi Arabia on 24 June 2011.[11] Also Alexandria Airlines launched its operations in 2007 with a fleet of Boeing 737-500s and sometimes leased aircraft for short periods. This airline limited its schedule to destinations in the Middle East (Amman, Kuwait, Jeddah).[12] And still in 2007, EgyptAir also had to face competition from Air Italy Egypt, which was created under the name Euro Mediterranean Airlines as a subsidiary of the Italian carrier, based in Egypt. Initially, the airline operated a single Boeing 757-200 that was later replaced by a Boeing 737-800. In September 2009, Euro Mediterranean Airlines was rebranded as Air Italy Egypt.[13] But when the parent company encountered financial difficulties, the Egyptian brand vanished.

AlMasria Universal Airlines

Plans to launch AlMasria Universal Airlines were announced in 2008 and operations launched in June 2009. According to Hassan Aziz, the CEO of the airline, the carrier would launch operations to take advantage of low prices during the global financial crisis to tap demand for air travel in Egypt, the most populous country in the Arab world. The airline started out with a fleet of two leased Airbus A320s, obtained from BOC Aviation. Plans called for another three A320s to join the fleet later on. In December 2009, AlMasria had become the first international airline to operate flights to Saudi Arabia's Yanbu airport, followed by flights to Qassim. Maintenance was out-sourced to EgyptAir under a total service agreement. The national carrier would also train AlMasria's crew and technical team, and the ground-handling would be performed by EgyptAir. Notwithstanding its cooperation with EgyptAir, AlMasria was also a potential competitor to EgyptAir, especially on routes to Saudi Arabia.[14]

Air Arabia Egypt

The most important competitor, however, was Air Arabia Egypt. Air Arabia was established on 3 February 2003 in Sharjah by Amiri decree, issued by Sultan bin Muhammad Al-Qasimi, the Ruler of Sharjah and member of the Supreme Council of the United Arab Emirates. Air Arabia was the first low-fare airline in the Middle East. The airline broke even during the first year of operation. Air Arabia soon started setting up subsidiaries in other Arab countries. On 9 September 2009, Air Arabia announced Air Arabia Egypt would be set up as a joint venture with Egyptian travel and tourism company Travco Group. The airline would be based in Alexandria. The carrier received its operating licence on 22 May 2010, with commercial flights beginning on 1 June that year. The fleet in Egypt, which consisted of Airbus A320s, offered scheduled service and charter traffic from Europe to the Red Sea.[15]

Increased competition from the new airlines that had entered the scene, combined with the fall out of the Arab Revolution, brought EgyptAir into a crisis situation. On 7 May 2013, when EgyptAir celebrated its 81st anniversary, the airline offered its customers numerous awards and discounts on their ticket prices. Within the celebration of this occasion, EgyptAir launched a contest 'Memories of

Egypt', in which clients were asked to post their photos, taken in tourist areas in Egypt. These photos were published on the official facebook page of EgyptAir. Friends and relatives were asked to vote for the best photos. Notwithstanding its problems, EgyptAir won Best Airline of the Year for Africa in the KLIA Awards in November 2013. These awards are an annual event organised by Malaysia Airports Holding. In June 2014, EgyptAir became the official carrier of the Pharaoh's Rally. The rally was organised by the Egyptian coastal town of el Gouna under the supervision of the Ministry of Tourism and in cooperation with the Automobile and Touring Club of Egypt.

EgyptAir received this Airbus A330-300 in 2011 while the Arab Revolution was affecting the carrier's operations. (Andrey Nesvetaev)

Airbus A330-300 SU-GDU was delivered in 2011. (Alan Bushell)

This Boeing 777 was delivered to EgyptAir wearing the Star Alliance paint scheme. (Allen Watkin from London, UK, CC BY-SA 2.0, via Wikimedia Commons)

Nile Air was one of the many new entrants in the market, prior to the Arab revolution. (Ken Fielding/https://www.flickr.com/photos/kenfielding, CC BY-SA 3.0, via Wikimedia Commons)

Nesma Airlines also entered the scene just prior to the Arab Spring. (Björn Strey CC BY-SA 2.0, via Wikimedia Commons)

Air Italy Egypt operated under the name Euro Mediterranean Airlines with this Boeing 757. (John Taggart from Sunbury on Thames, Middlesex, CC BY-SA 2.0, via Wikimedia Commons)

AlMasria started competing with EgyptAir. (Collection Jozef Mols)

Air Arabia Egypt was the most powerful competitor in the Egyptian market. (Björn Strey, CC BY-SA 2.0, via Wikimedia Commons)

Chapter 14

Restructuring

Given the mounting losses, EgyptAir had to consider a restructuring programme after facing a drop in occupancy rates to 62 per cent, and in revenues, which had declined at a much steeper rate of around 22 per cent due to eroding yields. As part of a new turnaround plan, the airline was planning network and capacity cuts. The plan anticipated a combination of network adjustments, more transit traffic and the start of a recovery in inbound tourist numbers, which was expected for 2015. As EgyptAir's new business plan envisioned an improvement in demand as political stability returned to Egypt, the capacity cuts were not expected to exceed ten per cent, however.[1]

While EgyptAir was planning to reduce total capacity by ten per cent, an adjustment in the fleet was not expected. Capt. Hefny, the new CEO of EgyptAir pointed out that the carrier had already dealt with excess fleet capacity by leasing two of its 777s to Biman Bangladesh, and five of its narrowbody aircraft to other Egyptian carriers. By the summer of 2014, the EgyptAir fleet consisted of 11 Airbus A320-200s, four Airbus A321-200s, seven A330-200s, four Airbus A330-300Es (including one on order), two Airbus A340-200s, 1 Boeing 737-500 (and three more in storage), 20 Boeing 737-800s, one Boeing 777-200ER in storage and six Boeing 777-300ERs.

The new business plan suggested transit traffic should be increased even though it was transit traffic that had historically eroded yields. Since the start of the political crisis, EgyptAir had increased its proportion of transit traffic, by 5 per cent to 35 per cent of the carrier's total traffic in 2014, up from about 17 per cent in 2013. But this growth had been achieved through heavy discounting, resulting in unsustainably low yields.[2]

In addition, a restructuring of the long-haul network was necessary, especially of the Asian routes. EgyptAir had already suspended its flights to Jakarta, which were only added in late 2013 with three weekly frequencies via Bangkok. Only 12 flights had been operated on the route, due to the MERS virus in Saudi Arabia, which impacted demand for Indonesians travelling to Saudi Arabia on religious pilgrim trips. As local demand between Egypt and Indonesia is very small, the Jakarta route was heavily dependent on transit passengers heading via Egypt to Saudi Arabia.[3] Traffic to Kuala Lumpur, which was also served via Bangkok, was also being reviewed as the route had been highly unprofitable. EgyptAir had pick-up-rights between Bangkok and Kuala Lumpur and relied heavily on these rights as Cairo to Kuala Lumpur traffic was very limited. However, demand on the local sector had dried up as a result of the political crisis in Thailand. Therefore, the carrier was reviewing opportunities to serve Kuala Lumpur via another destination including Mumbai. Routes to Beijing and Guangzhou, which were served non-stop from Cairo with five and three frequencies respectively, were performing much better than the Southeast Asian network.[4]

Flights to Europe, where EgyptAir served 20 destinations, had been impacted by the decline in inbound tourism following the Arab Revolution and by stiff competition in transit markets. Europe still accounted for about 20 per cent of EgyptAir's international seat capacity, but more cuts in the flight schedule were expected.[5]

The Middle East was EgyptAir's biggest market, with 18 destinations and 54 per cent of its international seat capacity. But EgyptAir had added too much capacity in the region, with a heavy reliance on transit traffic and connections with other Star Alliance carriers since Star did not have any other members in the Middle East. Having increased capacity on short-haul routes from 100,000 weekly seats in June 2011 to 130,000 in 2014 was too ambitious, especially as the Arab Revolution affected traffic in Egypt, and had spread to most other Arab countries. Therefore, where frequencies on some routes could be decreased, a few small unprofitable markets could be eliminated entirely.[6]

In the past, EgyptAir had also pursued expansion in Africa, but on a much smaller scale. Total international capacity to Africa had increased from about 23,000 weekly seats in June 2011 to about 42,000 seats in 2014. Destinations including Abidjan and Harare had been added to the timetable, and capacity to most North African countries had been increased. Now though, some destinations slated to be launched were removed from the business plan entirely, including N'Djamena in Chad, Mogadishu in Somalia, and Djibouti. Further growth in Africa was now set aside as the carrier focussed on recovery.[7]

The Russian market had been very important for the Egyptian tourism industry but as a result of the Arab Revolution, the Russian foreign ministry had urged tourists to avoid Egypt.[8] Russians instead travelled to Italy and Spain for leisure, but with the ruble buckling under the weight of Western sanctions and low oil prices, Egypt soon found favour with Russian tourists once more. In 2014, according to Russian sources, three million Russians visited Egypt, making up one-third of all visitors to the country. These were huge numbers for Egypt, which hadn't seen tourism rebound since the Arab Spring.[9] However, the massive influx of Russian tourists came to an abrupt end. On October 2015, a chartered flight operated by Russian airline Kogalymavia (branded as Metrojet), exploded above the northern Sinai Peninsula following its departure from Sharm el Sheikh International Airport en route to Pulkovo Airport, Saint Petersburg (Russia). All 224 passengers and crew on board were killed. Russian investigators concluded the cause of the crash was most likely the explosion of an onboard explosive device. Shortly after the tragedy, the Islamic State's Sinai branch, previously known as Anwar Bait al-Maqdis, claimed responsibility. British and US authorities also concluded the Airbus A321 had exploded due to a bomb. On 24 February 2016, the Egyptian president acknowledged that terrorism was the cause.[10] In November 2015, Russian authorities banned EgyptAir from flying to Russia, citing security concerns.

Shortly before the Metrojet disaster, rumours had spread that EgyptAir was negotiating with the Russian Sukhoi company for several Sukhoi SSJ-100 Superjets.[11] After the cancellation of the carrier's landing rights in Russia, the deal ended.

Not long after, EgyptAir was the victim of a major accident. On 18 May 2016, EgyptAir flight MS804 took off from Paris Charles de Gaulle Airport with 56 passengers and seven crew on board. In the early hours of May 19, the Airbus A320 (SU-GCC) had entered Egyptian airspace at an altitude of 37,000ft and crossed the KUMBI waypoint, and then contact was lost.[12] EgyptAir said that armed forces search-and-rescue personnel had received a distress signal from the aircraft's emergency devices. According to French investigators, an automated system aboard the plane had sent messages about smoke in the front of the cabin just before it crashed into the sea. After its departure from Paris, the Aircraft Communications Addressing and Reporting System (ACARS) that sends messages between planes and the ground had sent 11 electronic messages. The first two messages had indicated the engines worked normally. But the next messages stated a rise in the co-pilot's window temperature and about smoke in locations such as the lavatory and avionics compartment below the cockpit. Debris from the plane was later recovered, including life vests, personal belongings and parts of the wreckage.[13] Small fragments of human remains had also been found. Greek Defence Minister Panos Kammenos said that, when the aircraft had left Greek airspace and entered Egyptian airspace, it swerved 90 degrees left and then 360 degrees before plunging dramatically. After months of investigations, France's Bureau of Enquiry and Analysis for Civil Aviation Safety (BEA) concluded that pilot Mohamed Sai Shoikair's smoke break led to a fire on board the aircraft when his cigarette ignited oxygen leaking from an oxygen mask in the cockpit. The conclusion was, in part, supported by black box data that had captured the sound of oxygen hissing. EgyptAir's pilots were allowed to smoke in the cockpit – a rule that has since changed.[14] Egypt refused to release its own report into the crash and rejected BEA's findings, dismissing them as 'unfounded'.

Chapter 15
Fleet Renewal

The management of EgyptAir was fully aware of the challenges it would have to face. In the 2015-2016 Annual Report, the (then) CEO Safwat Mousallam underlined that the airline had to seek new opportunities with a focus on rebalancing the group portfolio. Therefore, it was necessary to implement a major restructuring plan, which included modernising the fleet, development of the network and the implementation of a cost reduction plan.

Of the EgyptAir group, it was mainly EgyptAir Airlines that was in need of restructuring; the other subsidiaries of the group were making profits. EgyptAir Express showed positive results as it achieved a profit of EGP 77m (£2.4m) in fiscal year 2015/2016 in comparison to EGP 2m (£63,000) a year earlier. The cargo division had managed to address the massive overcapacity in the market through launching services in other niche markets such as pharma product shipping: a new activity that was a good opportunity and a new challenge for the division in a bid to capitalise on a fast-growing and high-margin industry. EgyptAir Cargo hit a surplus of EGP 127m. (£4m) in 2015/16 compared to EGP 109m (£3.4m) the previous year, notwithstanding a decline in cargo volume. Export cargo traffic had dropped by six per cent to 77,806 tonnes while import cargo volume declined by nine per cent to 35,676 tonnes. EgyptAir Maintenance and Engineering had passed the periodic audits including those of the European Union Aviation Safety Agency in Cairo, Sharm el Sheikh and Borg El Arab. This way it could expand its services to the African and Asian markets within the field of aircraft heavy maintenance and overhaul. The division showed a profit of EGP 200m. (£6.2m) in comparison to the EGP 111m. (£3.5m) the previous year. EgyptAir Inflight Services recorded a profit of EGP 27m. (£847,000).[1] EgyptAir Airlines though published a deficit of EGP 1,279,655,040 (£40m)[2]

A developing plan for EgyptAir's fleet was set until the year 2021, including options of replacing and renewing aircraft or increasing seat capacity. As part of the plan, EgyptAir purchased nine Boeing 737-800s from Boeing in fiscal year 2015/16 with delivery dates starting from December 2016 until December 2017. Eight of the aircraft were financed by Sale & Lease Back with Dubai Aerospace Enterprise (DAE). The aircraft were provided with 16 business class seats and 138 economy class seats. Also, EgyptAir Cargo was planning a fleet renewal programme. In 2015, the company was operating one Airbus A300-B4F and two Airbus A300-600F aircraft. In order to reduce the high operational cost of the A300-B4, an agreement was concluded with EFW Elbe Flugzeugwerke to convert two Airbus A330-200s into cargo planes by mid 2018. The A300-B4 (SU-GAC) would be replaced by the end of 2017. At the same time, EgyptAir Cargo was planning to develop its fleet by adding one more A330-200 P2F aircraft by 2019 besides two short-range aircraft (probably Airbus A320) to enable the carrier to reach African markets. Under this development plan, the two A300-600Fs could be phased out. The plan would provide the carrier with 33 per cent additional payload once completed.

The presentation of a turn-around plan alone is not enough to turn losses into profits, and a positive evolution takes time before it shows in the bookkeeping. In fiscal year 2016/17, EgyptAir's losses increased to EGP 5,553,022,954 (£162m).[3] Nevertheless, the company could look back at some positive events in 2017, when the 85th anniversary was celebrated. The airline operated its first two all-female-crewed flights taking off from Cairo to Abu Dhabi and Kuwait. This happened in the framework of Egypt's celebration of Egyptian Woman's Day. In order to increase its presence in Africa, the airline signed a code-share agreement with Kenya Airways. This allowed customers to book through EgyptAir for Kenya Airways flights from Nairobi to Mombasa, Harare, Dar es Salaam, Lusaka while vice versa, Kenya Airlines customers could book EgyptAir flights from Cairo to Nairobi, Khartoum, Entebbe, Istanbul and vice versa. With Aegean Airlines, the code-share partnership was further expanded. A route from Cairo to Narita in Japan was opened, giving the Japanese tourists the opportunity to visit Egyptian tourist sites. Starting in April 2016, the airline added more than 50 weekly flights to several destinations in Saudi Arabia, boosting the number of weekly connections to 200. On some of these routes, wide-body aircraft were used. Every week, EgyptAir operated 84 flights to Jeddah, 42 flights to Medina, seven flights to Ahbha and Al Qassim, and 30 flights to Damam and Riyadh. To these flights from Cairo, several flights from other Egyptian airports were added.[4] EgyptAir also carried 200,000 pilgrims to Jeddah and Medina during the Umrah season. In-flight services were improved by adding a new service for the blind, deaf and hard of hearing people by providing them with entertainment in Arabic and English, as well as a Braille booklet containing useful information.

However, in January 2016, the US Department of Commerce's Bureau of Industry and Security (BIS) had fined EgyptAir $140,000 (£118,000) for leasing aircraft to Sudan Airways in breach of sanctions against the latter country. The fine followed an investigation triggered by EgyptAir having leased two Boeing 737-500s to Sudan Airways in 2010/11, breaching the US Export Administration Regulations. The lease was effectively a re-export of American airliners, according to BIS. Sudan had been under sanctions since 1997 because of its alleged support of terrorism and human rights abuses. As a result, Sudan Airways had increasingly struggled to maintain services and was forced to resort to leasing-in capacity.[5]

Then in June 2017, several EgyptAir flights to Doha in Qatar were delayed following an announcement by Egypt, Saudi Arabia, Bahrain and the United Arab Emirates that they were severing diplomatic ties with Qatar, accusing the Gulf state of supporting terrorism[6]. Egypt had announced the closure of its airspace and seaports for all Qatari transportation to protect its national security, the Egyptian foreign ministry said. Saudia, the flag carrier of Saudi Arabia, had also suspended its flights to Qatar and other airlines including Fly Dubai, Emirates, Etihad Airways and Air Arabia followed this move.

EgyptAir Cargo could publish much better results with a profit of EGP 201,630,197 (£6.3m) after operating 709 flights. Export cargo traffic had increased by 12 per cent while imports increased by nine per cent. This growth was the result of EgyptAir Cargo's decision to diversify its product portfolio to include products other than vegetables and fruits. Pharmaceutical products and high yield cargo loads were added.[7] The maintenance and engineering company had seen its profits rise to 260,624,995 (£8m). This growth came after opening new horizons in the African and Asian markets in the field of aircraft maintenance and overhaul. The company had signed a contract with Air Zimbabwe to carry out an overhaul on its A340 aircraft. It would also carry out the C-check of Air Madagascar's B737-800, as well as specific checks for the A320 of Nile Airlines.[8] This had resulted in a growth in third party revenue by 21.5 per cent.

EgyptAir In-Flight Services' 2,800 employees prepared eight million meals per year with an average of 20,000 meals per day for both EgyptAir flights, flights by other carriers, cafetarias and restaurants at Egyptian airports and transit hotels. It reported revenues of EGP 617m (£19m) resulting in a profit of EGP 73m (£2.2m). Considering these results, the company was planning the purchase of high-loaders. Furthermore, the catering units in Sharm el-Sheikh and Hurghada would be expanded. Solar energy would, in part, replace electric energy.[9]

Whereas several companies of the EgyptAir group were doing well, EgyptAir Airlines remained loss-making. The management fully understood fleet renewal was necessary to improve the image of the airline in the international market and to reduce the fuel consumption of the fleet, which was an important cost factor. Therefore, EgyptAir Holding Company started proceedings for securing the largest deal in the history of Egyptian aviation, which would see it receive 45 of the latest aircraft in a deal worth $6bn (£5bn). At the 2017 Dubai Air Show, a deal was signed with three major aircraft manufacturers: Boeing, Airbus and Bombardier.[10] The chairman of the EgyptAir Holding announced a long-term lease agreement for 15 Airbus A320Neo jets, provided by the AerCap leasing company. Delivery was scheduled for 2020. Furthermore, AerCap would also deliver six Boeing 787 Dreamliners. EgyptAir also signed an agreement with Canadian aircraft manufacturer Bombardier to purchase 12 C-300s (which would later be called the Airbus A220).

An EgyptAir Cargo Airbus A300 seen at the Ostend Airport in Belgium. (Collection Jozef Mols)

EgyptAir was planning to replace its cargo A300s with newer aircraft types. (Raymond Zamitt)

This Boeing 737-800 displays the logo designed to celebrate 85 years of EgyptAir. (Rodrigo Train Cortès)

The maintenance division made profits thanks to its activities in the African market. (EgyptAir)

The maintenance division takes care of the entire aircraft, as well as its subsystems. (EgyptAir)

The training academy uses the most advanced simulators. (EgyptAir)

Duty-free shops contributed to the group profits. (EgyptAir)

Chapter 16
Profits?

In an interview with Reuters in November 2017, EgyptAir's chairman Safwat Musallam was optimistic about the future of the airline.[1] According to the chairman, EgyptAir had struggled to rebound from the 2008 global financial crisis and two revolutions that had affected Egypt's economy, but he predicted a return to profitability in 2018. He said the airline would carry nine million passengers, compared to eight million in the previous year. He also stated the airline could reduce costs by reducing the workforce by about 500 employees (or 10 per cent) as staff who resigned would not be replaced. Furthermore, he stated the airline would start replacing its older Airbus A320 and A330 aircraft, as well as its Embraer jets in a move to reduce operating costs and fuel consumption. Unfortunately for him – and for the airline – his predictions proved to be wrong. In the fiscal year 2017/18, EgyptAir Airlines made a loss of EGP 1,915,445,094 (£58.3m), which was substantially less than the previous year (5.553 022 956 or £169m) but still a loss.[2]

Fortunately for EgyptAir Holding, other companies within the group booked better results. EgyptAir Maintenance and Engineering for example increased its profits to EGP 397,429,541 (£12.1m). EgyptAir Express, which had been in the red in 2016/17, showed a profit of EGP 43.215.910 (£1.3m). And EgyptAir Tourism more than tripled its profits to EGP 378,070,894 (£11.5m).[3] This came after the opening of revamped duty-free shopping and food and beverage outlets at the two new airports that opened in Egypt.[4] The new Sphinx International Airport is located on the Cairo-Alexandria desert road and shares some infrastructure with the Cairo West Air Base. By offering flights to this new airport, tourists may visit the pyramids without having to arrive at the busy Cairo International Airport. Sphinx opened in summer 2018, and commercial operations were set to start in October 2018, but it would take until January 2020 before the first international flight landed. This was operated by Fly Jordan. Plans are already underway to expand the airport complex.[5] At the same time that the construction of Sphinx airport began, a new airport, located approximately 45km (28 miles) east of Cairo was under construction. This facility was inaugurated by the President of Egypt on 9 July 2019. The airport will handle business flights, training flights and regional flights, taking away traffic from the congested Cairo International Airport.[6]

EgyptAir Ground Services saw its profits drop to EGP 95,623,422 (£2.9m), and also profits of EgyptAir Cargo saw a decline to EGP 176,856,586 (£5.4m). Nevertheless, there was also some good news for EgyptAir's chairman. Direct flights between Cairo and Moscow resumed after two years on 12 April 2018. EgyptAir would operate this route by Airbus A320 three times a week. Egypt agreed to the Russian request to station Russian security personnel at Cairo airport where the EgyptAir and Aeroflot flights would depart.[7] To further expand its presence in Europe, EgyptAir and TAP Portugal also expanded their codeshare on European routes. The new agreement enabled EgyptAir to put its MS code on TAP flights from Lisbon to Amsterdam Schiphol, London Heathrow, Frankfurt and Munich, Geneva and Vienna. In exchange, TAP would add the MS code on flights including Amsterdam-Porto and Porto-Vienna.[8] With LOT Polish Airlines, a codeshare partnership was started from November 2017 onward. EgyptAir would put its MS code on Warsaw-Budapest and Warsaw-Milan Malpensa flights, operated by LOT. LOT would put its code on flights between Cairo and Budapest and Cairo and Milan Malpensa. The existing codeshare agreement with Etihad Airways was enhanced to include more destinations in Africa, North Asia and Australia.

About a year after Safwat Musallam made his prediction, the airline became profitable again, Over the 2018/19 period, passenger numbers increased to 7,809,202, up four per cent from 7.5m in the previous fiscal year. All routes showed a growth, except for flights within the Middle East, which saw a decrease in passenger numbers of 4.3 per cent. Traffic in the Middle East still accounted for 48 per cent of all passengers transported. Load factors on all routes had increased by six per cent.[9] The airline reported a modest profit of EGP 279,473,849 (£8.5m), the first positive result in ten years. EgyptAir's Duty Free subsidiary showed the largest percentage increase with a profit of EGP 457m (£13.9m), and the inflight service department results remained stable. EgyptAir's Maintenance and Engineering Co saw its profits drastically decline by more than 50 per cent and the same happened to EgyptAir Express. This was mainly due to heavy investments and increasing wages. The cargo department also saw a small decline in its profits.

During 2018/19, EgyptAir had received three Boeing 787-9 Dreamliners. The airline had carried 120,000 pilgrims to Saudi Arabia on more than 450 flights including pilgrims from Palestine and Mali. New flights to Washington, Kigali and Abidjan were introduced. And the airline had concluded a codeshare partnership with China's Shenzhen Airlines on its Cairo-Guangzhou route. EgyptAir Cargo had introduced its second Airbus A330-200 after being converted from a passenger aircraft to a P2F cargo aircraft. These aircraft were immediately put to work on cargo routes to South Africa and Bombay in India. EgyptAir had selected Flight Safety International to design and manufacture a full flight simulator for the Airbus A220-300 aircraft it had ordered. Also a new A320 Reality Seven Full Flight Simulator was ordered. The maintenance and engineering division had signed a contract to establish a centre for technical services to serve airlines operating from and to Kotoko International Airport in Accra, Ghana.

The optimism with which the 2018/19 annual report was published would soon disappear when, by the end of 2019, the COVID-19 pandemic began to spread around the world. Coronavirus had a great impact on aviation around the world, considering the duration and magnitude of the outbreak, containment measures and economic implications. Airlines in many countries would be forced to ground their fleets and tourism came to a stand still. It became clear that EgyptAir, would have to implement a new restructuring programme to survive this new crisis.

As a result of the COVID-19 pandemic, and the airline's results over previous years, a study was published at the end of 2019.[10] After a descriptive analysis of the strategic turnaround decisions and the restructuring programme the airline had carried out in the past, the authors presented suggestions for further restructuring. It was suggested that Egypt Airlines merge with EgyptAir Express and the flight operations of EgyptAir Cargo into one entity under the name EgyptAir Airlines. At the same time, EgyptAir Holding should increase its stake in Air Cairo from 60 per cent to 100 per cent in order to change its business model from a charter carrier with part scheduled operation to a low-cost carrier within the group. Furthermore, a shift of the passenger handling activities, the cargo warehouse from EgyptAir Cargo, the cabin cleaning and aircraft push back services from EgyptAir Maintenance to Air Ground Services would provide a more efficient full package ground-handling service to in-house subsidiaries and third-party clients. As for EgyptAir Holding it should concentrate on corporate strategy and planning, rather than incorporating operational activities such as security, construction and facilities management, which should be transferred to EgyptAir Supplementary Industries. The authors concluded that the past problems of the airline were the result of political upheaval, and that the Egyptian government should inject a one-time public subsidy into EgyptAir to support fulfilling its financial obligations and the strategic turnaround plan. Once this turnaround was achieved, the authors advised EgyptAir to seek a strategic partnership with a global carrier, which might include an equity share.

In November 2019, news company Almal News published a report that EgyptAir Holding Company had accepted the idea of merging cargo transportation activities with EgyptAir Airlines, as well as transforming Air Cairo into a low-cost arm of EgyptAir. The holding company would be transformed into a strategic entity, according to the recommendations of the study. Furthermore, EgyptAir announced it would complete the development of a revenue and pricing management structure, to adjust the structure of the different sales channels and to implement a further fleet modernisation plan between 2021 and 2027.[11, 12]

As a result of the fleet modernisation plan, EgyptAir leased two more Boeing 787-9 aircraft from AerCap Holdings, the first of which was scheduled for delivery in 2021 and the second would arrive in 2022. The announcement of the deal was made during the 2019 Dubai Airshow.[13] Earlier, EgyptAir had written history by being the first carrier to operate a Boeing 787 powered by bio-fuel. The aircraft flew from Seattle to Cairo on a delivery flight.[14] Also during the Dubai Airshow, it was announced EgyptAir had reached agreement with AerCap concerning the conversion of seven previously executed leases for Airbus aircraft. The signed documents of the agreement converted seven leases for Airbus A320neos into leases for seven Airbus A321neos.[15]

Still in line with the restructuring programme, EgyptAir Express was completely merged with EgyptAir and would continue to operate the Embraer E170, which would, however, gradually be sold at a rate of one per month. The aircraft would be replaced by Airbus A220s, operated by EgyptAir mainline. As EgyptAir was planning to achieve integration between its own flight schedules and those of EgyptAir Express, code-share agreements between the two entities were signed. Former Air Cairo would place its flight code on domestic flights, now operated by EgyptAir, as well as on international flights between Cairo and Rome, Milan, Bahrain and Copenhagen.[16]

EgyptAir Cargo introduced the Airbus A330-200 (P2F) (Colin Cooke Photo, CC BY-SA 2.0, via Wikimedia Commons)

Above: The Boeing 787-9 Dreamliners entered the fleet in fiscal year 2018/19. (N509FZ, CC BY-SA 4.0, via Wikimedia Commons)

Left: EgyptAir added two 787-9s to its leased fleet during the Dubai Air Show. (Raymond Zamitt)

Below: The passenger version of the Airbus A330 disappeared from the fleet. (Andrey Nesvetaev)

Chapter 17

EgyptAir Today

The period between 2017 and 2020 was in many respects very significant for EgyptAir. Between March and August 2019, the carrier received a total of six Boeing B787-9s. Five Airbus A320neos arrived between February and June 2020 followed by 12 Airbus A220-300 between September 2019 and September 2020. With these new arrivals, EgyptAir had become the first carrier in mainland Africa and the Middle East to operate the Airbus A320neo and Airbus A220. It was difficult to put all these new aircraft in service, as the COVID-19 pandemic forced EgyptAir to cancel several flights. Recently opened routes to Douala in Cameroon and Huangzhou in China also had to be suspended. On 19 March 2020, the airline suspended all scheduled passenger flights as part of the pandemic response. Fortunately, it managed to delay the delivery dates of two Boeing 787-9s for a period of one year. Deliveries were rescheduled to take place in November 2022 and February 2023. EgyptAir Cargo had received the third and last Airbus A330-200 after conversion from a commercial passenger aircraft into a cargo aircraft.

As a result of the pandemic, EgyptAir had to determine a plan for storing the operating aircraft in its fleet. Some passenger aircraft were kept out of storage with the implementation of at least one flight weekly for each one whenever possible. They were used to repatriate Egyptian nationals stranded abroad (for which 11 flights were operated), as well as to evacuate foreign nationals residing in Egypt. EgyptAir training courses in various fields were changed from classroom-teaching to digital learning.

In June 2020, it became known that EgyptAir had been losing almost $200m (£165m) a month since it was grounded in mid-March. As a result, the airline had to seek a loan of $185m (£153m) from state-owned banks to help it survive the crisis. Part of the funds were needed to pay foreign loans the airline had taken to purchase new aircraft. At the time the airline started to negotiate the loans, it was operating at 20 to 30 per cent of its capacity. It was hoped it would return to 50 per cent by the end of 2020 … if tourists would return to Egypt. In May 2020, EgyptAir received $127.39m (£105m) from the government to help the carrier weather the crisis. According to the country's finance ministry, the government would continue to support the carrier until it returned to 80 per cent of its 2019 operation. The International Air Transport Association said that Egypt had witnessed a decrease in the number of passengers equivalent to 13 million passengers. Without aid Egypt would have suffered revenue losses of around $2.2bn (£18.1bn), placing 279,800 jobs in danger.[1] EgyptAir had a workforce of 20,500 people at the time of the crisis.

As a result of increased sanitary measures during the pandemic, all planes were sterilised, only canned drinks and dry foods were served and inflight magazines were banned. In an attempt to encourage tourists to return to Egypt, the country had waived tourist visas for key resorts, and museums and historical places offered ticket discounts of 20 per cent. For airlines, the government had put in place a ten per cent discount on every gallon of jet fuel purchased from government-owned fuel suppliers and reduced landing and boarding fees by 50 per cent. Ground services were also discounted by 20 per cent.[2] EgyptAir migrated its Duty-Free operations to IBM Cloud and leverage IBM Watson Assistant to help transform travellers' retail experience. This would allow EgyptAir Duty-Free customers to do online shopping through the Duty-Free website including placing orders, payment and delivery inside the plane. With the COVID-19 pandemic, airlines around the world started to look for new technologies to reinvent their services and unlock an array of new experiences for their customers, and EgyptAir followed this trend.³

The annual report of EgyptAir over 2019/2020 revealed EgyptAir Airlines had a loss of EGP 2,425,212,858 (£67.2m). EgyptAir Cargo had a modest profit of EGP 31,409,808 (£871,000). EgyptAir Ground Services went in the red with a loss of EGP 159,250,259 (£4.4m). So too did Maintenance and Engineering Co with a loss of EGP 105,861,651 (£2.9m).And as flights were suspended (except some repatriation flights and domestic operations), EgyptAir Inflight Services also booked a loss of EGP 16,989,326 (£470,500). If the Cargo division had been able to make a profit, this was as a result of the initial demand for transporting medical supplies, leading the division to temporarily convert some grounded passenger aircraft into freighters. Despite the global lockdown, the pandemic had also highlighted the urgent need for air cargo to follow the global transition to eCommerce.⁴

In October 2020, EgyptAir reached agreement with the government of Ghana to set up a Ghanaian national aviation company with investment from both the Egyptian and Ghanaian governments. This happened after a similar earlier deal between Ghana and Ethiopian Airlines fell through. The new company would launch its lines across Africa, connecting it with countries of North and South America. EgyptAir previously cooperated with Ghana in 2018, when EgyptAir Maintenance and Engineering established a technical service centre for airlines operating to and from Kotoka International Airport in Accra. Ghana had been without a national airline since the collapse of Ghanaian International Airlines.⁵

In the past, flights between Egypt and Israel were operated by Air Sinai (a subsidiary of EgyptAir) in unmarked Airbus A220 planes. EgyptAir started to operate commercial flights linking Cairo and Tel Aviv in October 2021. The airline indicated it would operate four weekly flights.⁶

EgyptAir started its recovery in 2022. Flights to Toronto and Bangkok resumed by the end of February. A route to Kinshasa was opened by March 27 with three flights per week, and a new route to Dublin became operational in June with four flights per week, operated by Airbus A320neo. At the same time, EgyptAir started talks with the government of Sudan (once an Egyptian protectorate) to intensify cooperation in the field of civil aviation.⁷ In August 2022, an Egyptair plane landed in the Libyan capital for the first time after an eight year pause in air travel between the two countries. EgyptAir had ceased its operations after an uprising in Libya had ousted president Muammar Qaddafi, which resulted in more than a decade of civil war. Flights were expected to operate once a week between Sharm el Sheikh International Airport and Mitiga International Airport in Tripoli. The flights would be carried out by Boeing 737-800, which can carry up to 154 passengers.⁸ At the same time, EgyptAir and Libyan Airlines concluded an agreement regarding further cooperation. EgyptAir Training Academy would train Libyan Airlines pilots on the Airbus A320 and A330 models, as well as the cabin crew and engineers.⁹

Although EgyptAir was recovering from the pandemic, there was bad news ahead. On 5 March 2022, the airline had to cancel all flights to Moscow due to problems with European flight insurance. Insurance contracts had to be re-negotiated, and some European parties refused to insure flights to and from Moscow amid the events around the Russian invasion of Ukraine and the European sanctions against Russia.¹⁰ Shortly afterwards, EgyptAir announced it would resume daily flights to Moscow, beginning 15 April. In the absence of European insurance, Egyptian president Abdel-Fattah el-Sisi had ordered the finance ministry to offer an insurance guarantee to EgyptAir to fulfil its financial obligations in the event of an accident or the risks of the ongoing Russia-Ukraine war.¹¹ By the end of the year, Egyptair increased direct flights between Moscow and the Red Sea resort cities of Sharm el-Sheikh and Hurghada to 28 per week, starting in 2023, up from ten flights previously. The increase in flight numbers came following a move by Jordan a week earlier to close its airspace to Russian airlines due to sanctions against Russia. Egypt would be able to boost international tourist arrivals from Russia. Earlier, the country had already embarked on a vigorous campaign to market the country as a favourable destination. Articles about new archeological finds in Egypt were published, hoping to attract visitors from all over the world. According to Russian tour bookings agency Travelata, Egypt was among the top five tourist destinations for Russian tourists in the summer of 2022. The North African country came in the fourth place with four per cent of Russian tourist inflow after Russian resorts (55 per cent), Turkey (33 per cent) and Abkhazia (seven per cent).[12] While the Egyptian tourism sector – and EgyptAir – were hoping to see large numbers of tourists return to the country after the pandemic, the new EgyptAir CEO, Yehia Zakaria, pointed out that fleet modernisation was a top priority for his airline. In May 2022, the carrier had ordered a single Boeing 737-800 Freighter to supplement its existing fleet of widebody freighters. EgyptAir would convert one of its own 737-800s to a cargo plane to be used on short- and medium-haul flights.[13] This happened at the same time new passenger aircraft – including Airbus A321neo and Boeing 787-9 continued to strengthen the fleet.

Air Cairo (in which EgyptAir has a 60 per cent stake) also started to modernise its fleet. In November 2022, it was announced the airline had plans to induct an unspecified number of Embraer E190s after opening recruitment for pilots for the type.[14] The first three of these aircraft arrived in January 2023 and were leased through CIAF Leasing.[15] Earlier, Air Cairo had ordered six ATR 72-600s, to be used on short-haul routes These were leased from Nordic Aviation Capital. With the arrival of the first three ATRs, Air Cairo's fleet reached 17 aircraft including the three new planes plus 14 Airbus neo/ceo jets.[16] While Air Cairo was operating flights with a lower ticket price than EgyptAir, it was announced in mid-July 2022 the Egyptian government was considering setting up a low-cost carrier (LCC) by late 2022. This would be the first LCC in Egypt, and Air Sphinx (as the carrier would be named) would be a full subsidiary of EgyptAir. The new LCC would fly out of five key hubs, including Cairo International Airport, Hurghada International Airport, Sharm el Sheikh International Airport, Luxor International Airport and the new Sphinx International Airport, near Cairo.[17]

Did the fleet expansion and the increase in tourists from Russia prove EgyptAir had weathered the COVID? Fluctuations in tourism have always influenced the airline, so one can ask what will happen as a result of the Russia-Ukraine war? Today the impact of the war remains unclear. How will the worldwide energy crisis and the galloping inflation caused by the war influence the tourism sector? During the COVID-pandemic, EgyptAir managed to compensate losses in the passenger transportation sector by increasing profits from air cargo operations. But if the Russia-Ukraine war results in economic recession, both tourism and cargo operations may decline again.

An EgyptAir Express Embraer 170LR, operating an Air Sinai flight, seen during landing at David Ben Gurion Airport in Israel. (Oyoyoy, CC BY-SA 3.0, via Wikimedia Commons)

An EgyptAir Airbus A320neo in flight. (Gonçalo Guimaraes)

EgyptAir was the first carrier in Africa and the Middle East to introduce the Airbus A220. (Mztourist, CC BY-SA 4.0, via Wikimedia Commons)

EgyptAir's subsidiary Air Cairo leased a fleet of ATR-aircraft for short-haul operations. (ATR Aircraft)

Appendix 1
Incidents and Accidents

(Information from the Aviation Safety Network)

Misrair

On 22 December 1951, SNCASE Languedoc SU-AHH crashed west of Tehran, killing all 20 people on board. The aircraft was operating an international scheduled flight from Baghdad to Tehran.

On 30 July 1952, SNCASE Languedoc SU-AHX was damaged beyond economic repair in a wheels-up landing at Almaza Air Base in Cairo. The aircraft was operating an international scheduled passenger flight from Almaza to Khartoum Airport in Sudan. It returned to Cairo following a fire in No.1 engine. All 38 people on board survived.

United Arab Airlines

On 29 December 1960, Vickers Viscount SU-AKW crashed near Elba.

Flight 738 took off from Geneva flying to Cairo via Rome and Athens. At FL210 (Flight Level 210 or 21,000ft), the crew requested a change of heading to avoid unfavourable weather. The last contact made with the airline was when Rome air traffic control (ATC) cleared the aircraft for this change of heading. The aircraft crashed into the Tyrrhenian Sea off the island of Elba. The probable cause of the accident was determined as 'entry of the aircraft into a severe thunderstorm', which resulted in loss of control. All 21 people on board perished.

On 19 July 1962, de Havilland Comet 4C SU-AMW crashed near Bangkok. Flight 869 had departed from Hong Kong for Bangkok, an intermediate stop on a scheduled flight to Cairo. At 15.14 the pilot advised Bangkok ATC that the flight had crossed the Bangkok FIR boundary at 15.08 and passed over Ubol NDB at 15.13 and requested to fly direct from Ubol NDB to Bangkok VOR. This request was granted by Bangkok ATC. Then, the pilot advised Bangkok ATC that the ETA for Bangkok VOR would be 15.47. At 15.27 the flight advised Bangkok ATC that it would be over the 100-mile perimeter at 15.30. After reporting that it was 90 miles out the crew requested descent clearance to a lower altitude. Bangkok control cleared the flight to descend to 4,000ft on the Bangkok VOR radial of 073 degrees and to report when commencing descent from 31,000ft. The flight was instructed to contact Bangkok approach control at 15.39. At 15.35 the flight was cleared to 3,000ft and informed that the altimeter setting was 1007.8mb. At 15.40, the flight transferred to the Bangkok approach control. Immediately after this, the pilot reported to approach control that he was descending from 13,000ft and estimating Bangkok VOR at 15.44. Approach control advised the flight to adjust the altimeter setting to 1007.8mb and then cleared the flight to cross Bangkok VOR for final approach on runway 21R and report immediately on descending from 3,000ft. This was the last contact with the flight which flew into the side of Khao Yai Mountain, some 52nm north east of Bangkok. The principal cause of the accident was the pilot's action in commencing descent at 15.30 hours when the aircraft was 137 miles and not 90 miles from the Bangkok VOR as reported to Bangkok ATC, and the aircraft therefore collided with a mountain at a point 52 miles distant. It is probable that the pilot-in-command did not actually pass over the point he reported, but only estimated he had passed three points, which resulted in grave errors in time and distance in his computations.

On 15 May 1962, a Douglas DC-3 SU-AJM crashed shortly after take-off from Cairo on a flight to Beirut. While climbing, the aircraft went out of control and crashed near the runway end. All three crew were killed.

On 27 July 1963, de Havilland Comet, flight 869, crashed into the sea on approach to Bombay Airport, killing all 62 passengers and crew on board.

On 2 February 1966, an Antonov AN-24 SU-AOB crashed in Luxor during a test flight and was written off.

On 18 March 1966 Antonov An-24, flight 749, crashed while attempting to land at Cairo International Airport. All 30 passengers and crew on board were killed.

On 30 September 1966, Antonov AN-24, SU-AOM, crashed at Cairo Airport. The Antonov was preparing for take-off at Luxor when a camel entered the runway. The pilot deviated slightly to the right and tried to lift off quickly. The right undercarriage leg, however, struck the animal. As a result, the right gear leg couldn't be retracted. The crew flew on to Cairo, where a wheels-up landing was carried out on a sand strip next to the runway. There were no fatalities but the aircraft was damaged beyond repair.

On 18 August 1968, Antonov AN-24, SU-AOL from Cairo to Damascus crashed into the sea shortly after entering the Nicosia Flight Information Region. All 40 people on board perished.

On 20 March 1969, a, Ilyushin Il-18, SU-APC crashed while attempting to land at Aswan Airport. Rising sand in the Aswan area had caused visibility to drop from 10km (6.2 miles) to 2 or 3km (1¼–2 miles). The flight had missed two approaches to Aswan Airport and was approaching for the third time when it suddenly banked right. The right wing contacted the left side of the runway 1,120m (3,675ft) from the threshold. The wing broke off and the aircraft crashed in flames. The pilot had decended below the minimum safe altitude without having the runway lights clearly in sight. A contributory factor was fatigue arising from continuous working hours without suitable rest periods. One hundred of the 105 people on board were killed.

On 30 January 1970, Antonov AN-24, SU-AOK was damaged beyond repair at Luxor airport after the undercarriage collapsed on landing. There were no victims.

On 14 March 1970, an Antonov AN-24 SU-AOC crashed while operating a flight from Athens to Cairo with an en route stop at Alexandria. The no.1 propeller had to be feathered when, four minutes after take-off, an explosion occurred in the engine nacelle. The pilot continue to the destination (Cairo) where the gear and flaps could not be lowered so the aircraft made a wheels-up landing on the sand at the side of the runway. There were no victims but the aircraft was written off.

On 19 July 1970, Antonov AN-24 SU-ANZ on a training flight crashed at Cairo Airport. The Antonov returned for a series of five touch and goes. After the fifth landing with full stop, the aircraft took off and climbed steeply and then banked to the right with the no.2 propeller feathered. The bank angle increased to 90 degrees causing the aircraft to stall and crash. All three occupants were killed. The probable cause of the accident was incorrect action of the pilot under training and delayed corrective action by the pilot in command which led to the loss of control.

On 2 January 1971, a Comet, SU-ALC hit sand dunes on approach to Tripoli with the loss of eight passengers and eight crew.

EgyptAir

On 19 March 1972, McDonnell Douglas DC-9-32 YU-AHR, flight 763, flying from Cairo to Aden, crashed into a mountain on visual approach to Aden International Airport in Yemen, killing all 30 passengers and crew on board.

On 29 January 1973, Ilyushin IL-18D SU-AOV, flight 741, flying from Cairo to Nicosia, crashed into the Kyrenia Mountain range near the village of Karavas on approach to Nicosia International Airport during a downwind night-time approach, killing all 37 people on board.

On 10 July, 1974, a Tupolev TU-154 (SU-AXB) on a training flight crashed near Cairo Airport, killing four Soviet instructors and two EgyptAir pilots.

On 25 December 1976, Boeing 707 SU-AXA, flight 864 crashed into an industrial complex in Bangkok. All 52 people on board plus 19 people on the ground were killed.

On 17 October 1982, Boeing 707 SU-APE, flight 771, flying from Cairo crashed on landing at Geneva Airport. There were no fatalities but the aircraft was damaged beyond repair.

On 10 October 1985, a Boeing 737, flight 2843, carrying individuals responsible for the Achille Lauro hijacking was intercepted by American war planes and forced to land in Sigonella (Italy) while en route to Tunisia.

On 23 November 1985, Boeing 737, flight 648 to Malta International Airport was hijacked by three men from the Abu Nidal terrorist group. An Egyptian sky marshall on board shot and killed one of the hijackers before being gunned down. After several hours of negotiations, Egyptian troops stormed the aircraft and battled with the hijackers who threw hand grenades and shot and killed five passengers. The aircraft was severely damaged by the explosions and fire. Two of the six crew and 59 of the 90 passengers were killed.

On 21 September 1987, Airbus A300 SU-BCA crashed at Luxor International Airport during a training flight, killing all five crew. The Airbus had touched down 700m (2,300ft) past the runway threshold. The right main gear hit runway lights and the aircraft collided with an antenna and fences.

On 31 October 1999, Boeing 767 SU-GAP, flight 990, en route from Los Angeles to Cairo with a stopover in New York City, crashed into the Atlantic Ocean off the coast of Nantucket. All 219 passengers were killed. The relief first officer of the flight, Gameel Al-Batouti, was suspected by US authorities of making flight control inputs that led to the crash, though it could not be determined why he would have done this. Egyptian officials strongly disputed this claim.

On 7 May 2002, Boeing 737-500, flight 843, crashed into terrain in heavy rain, fog and a sandstorm on its approach to Tunis, killing 15 of 64 passengers and crew.

On 29 July 2011, Boeing 777-200, SU-GBP, flight 667, sustained substantial damage in a cockpit fire at Cairo International Airport. The probable cause of the accident was identified as an electrical fault or circuit. All passengers and crew escaped. The aircraft was damaged beyond repair.

Incidents and Accidents

On 29 March 2016, Airbus A320-200, SU-GCB, flight 181, was hijacked while on a flight from Borg El Arab Airport, Alexandria to Cairo International Airport. The aircraft, with 81 passengers on board, landed at Larnaca International Airport, where all hostages were released and the hijacker surrendered to authorities.

On 19 May 2016, Airbus A320-200 SU-GCC, flight 804, en route from Paris to Cairo crashed into the Mediterranean Sea. All 66 people on board were killed. The cause of the accident remains unclear, although the BEA believes that faulty maintenance led to fire, which rapidly spread across the plane leading to loss of control.

This Boeing 737-200 was involved in the Malta hijacking. (Raymond Zamitt)

Appendix 2
EgyptAir Fleet Details

(Based on information from eng.wikipedia.org, planespotters net and the airline)

Historic fleet

Aircraft type	Total	First introduced	Last removed
McDonnell Douglas DC-9-30	2	1971	1973
Boeing 737-200	11	1975	1999
Douglas DC-8-30	3	1976	1979
Douglas DC-8-20	2	1978	1979
Airbus A300-B4	10	1978	2018
Boeing 747-100	1	1983	1984
Boeing 767-200	4	1984	1997
Boeing 747-200	7	1984	1989
Douglas DC-8-30/70	2	1985	1989
Boeing 747-300	2	1988	2005
Airbus A300-C4-600	1	1988	1989
Lockheed L-1010 Tristar	2	1989	1990
Boeing 767-300	3	1989	2001
Airbus A300-600	10	1990	2019
Airbus A320-200	13	1991	2020
Boeing 737-500	5	1991	2017
Airbus A340-300	1	1995	1997
Airbus A340-200	3	1996	2015
Airbus A321-200	4	1997	2018
Boeing 777-200	5	1997	2018
Airbus A330-200	2	2005	2020
Embraer ERJ170	12	2007	2020

Current fleet (June 2022)

Aircraft type	Total	First delivery
Airbus A320-200	1	2003
Airbus A330-200	2	2005
Boeing 737-800	28	2006
Airbus A330-300	4	2010
Boeing 777-300ER	6	2010
Airbus A330-200F	3	2018
Airbus A220-300	12	2019
Boeing 787-9 Dreamliner	6	2019
Airbus A320neo	8	2020

Appendix 3

Notes and References

Chapter 1
1. 'Imperial Airways', eng.wikipedia.org
2. Abed, Sally, 'The first Egyptian aviators: a brief history', english.ahram.org.eg, 6 February 2022
3. ibid
4. ibid
5. 'The first aviation meeting in Africa', thefirstairraces.net. author unknown, date of publication unknown
6. 'Almaza Air Force Base', eng.wikipedia.org

Chapter 2
1. 'Misr Airlines – Arab Aviation in the '50s – Part 1' utopiaairport.blogspot.com, 7 June 2017, author unknown
2. 'Misr Airwork' eng.wikipedia.org
3. 'Misr Airlines – Arab Aviation in the '50s – Part 1', utopiaairport.blogspot.com, 7 June 2017, author unknown
4. ibid
5. 'Misr Airwork', eng.wikipedia.org
6. ibid
7. 'Egyptair', eng.wikipedia.org
8. 'Misr Airlines – Arab Aviation in the '50s – Part 2', utopiaairport.blogspot.com, 7 June 2017, author unknown
9. 'SAIDE', de.wikipedia.org
10. ibid

Chapter 3
1. '1948 Palestine War', eng.wikipedia.org
2. 'Egyptian Revolution of 1952', eng.wikipedia.org
3. ibid
4. 'Misr Airlines – Arab Aviation in the '50s – Part 2', utopiaairport.blogspot.com, 7 June 2017, author unknown
5. ibid
6. 'Suez Canal crisis', eng.wikipedia.org
7. 'Gamal Abdel Nasser', eng.wikipedia.org

Chapter 4
1. 'The Non-Aligned Movement', eng.wikipedia.org
2. 'United Arab Republic', eng.wikipedia.org
3. 'Syrian Air', eng.wikipedia.org
4. 'United Arab Airlines Vickers Viscount Services', utopiaairport.blogspot.com, 7 June 2017, author unknown
5. 'EgyptAir', eng.wikipedia.org

Notes and References

Chapter 5
1. 'Tripartite Declaration of 1950', eng.wikipedia.org
2. 'Aswan Dam', eng.wikipedia.org
3. ibid
4. 'Six Day War', eng.wikipedia.org
5. Gamal Abdel Nasser', eng.wikipedia.org
6. ibid
7. 'EgyptAir, eng.wikipedia.org
8. ibid

Chapter 6
1. 'EgyptAir', eng.wikipedia.org
2. 'Yom Kippur War', eng.wikipedia.org
3. 'Egyptair', eng.wikipedia.org
4. 'Egyptian Parliamentary Group studies accusation of a Boeing pay-off to airline', author unknown, nytime.com, 20 February 1976
5. Lippman, Thomas W, 'Egyptian aide alleges Boeing pay-offs', washingtonpost.com, 25 January 1977
6. Egypt indicts plane buyers', nytimes.com, 24 November 1978
7. 'EgyptAir', eng.wikipedia.org

Chapter 7
1. 'Egyptair', eng.wikipedia.org
2. 'Air Sinai', eng.wikipedia.org
3. Staff, Tol, 'First EgyptAir flight between Cairo and Tel Aviv lands at Ben Gurion Airport', 3 October 2021, The Times of Israel
4. Telushkin, Shira, 'The ghost airline that has linked Cairo and Tel Aviv for decades. Air Sinai is shrouded in mystery. But why?' atlasobscura.com, 23 April 2020
5. ibid
6. ibid
7. Martin, Patrick, 'Hush hush on Egypt's phantom flights to Egypt', theglobalandmail.com, 8 September 2011
8. 'Air Sinai', eng.wikipedia.org

Chapter 8
1. 'EgyptAir: International airline with a history of hijackings', cnn.com, 29 March 2016
2. 'The Achille Lauro hijacking', eng.wikipedia.org
3. Bohn, Michael K, *The Achille Lauro Hijacking: Lessons in the Politics and Prejudice of Terrorism.* 2004, Washington, D.C., Potomac Books, Inc
4. The Achille Lauro hijacking', eng.wikipedia.org
5. ibid
6. ibid
7. ibid
8. Bohn, Michael K, *The Achille Lauro Hijacking: Lessons in the Politics and Prejudice of Terrorism.* 2004, Washington, D.C., Potomac Books, Inc

Chapter 9
1. 'EgyptAir – pioneer of air travel', news.bbc.co.uk, 7 May 2002
2. 'Orders grow for 777s but 1995 deliveries show decline, flightglobal.com, 30 August 1995
3. Mc Murtry, Ian, 'Logo lineage part 6: North African flare', 30 May 2019, airlinegeeks.com
4. 'EgyptAir flight 990', eng.wikipedia.org
5. ibid
6. ibid
7. ibid
8. ibid

Chapter 10
1. 'EgyptAir company profile and history', Institute of Developing Economies, Japan External Trade Organization, ide.go.jp
2. 'EgyptAir divides operations into six in effort to multiply earnings', flightglobal.com, 9 July 2002,
3. Allam, Abeer, 'EgyptAir chairman ousted amid mounting criticism', nytimes.com, 18 June 2002
4. 'EgyptAir restructures its fleet', meed.com, 11 August 2003
5. 'EgyptAir', eng.wikipedia.org
6. 'EgyptAir chief replaced as losses continue', moodiedavittreport.com, 13 July 2003
7. 'EgyptAir restructures its fleet', meed.com, 11 August 2003
8. ibid

Chapter 11
1. 'Air Cairo', eng.wikipedia.org
2. 'AMC Airlines', eng.wikipedia.org
3. 'Lotus Air', eng.wikipedia.org
4. 'Midwest Airlines (Egypt)', eng.wikipedia.org
5. 'Tristar Air', eng.wikipedia.org
6. 'EgyptAir Company Profile and History', Institute of Developing Economies, Japan External Trade Organization, ide.go.jp
7. Dunn, Graham, 'Star Alliance entry to fuel EgyptAir expansion', flightglobal.com, 23 October 2007
8. 'Government scraps EgyptAir privatisation', flightglobal.com, 4 December 2007

Chapter 12
1. *Annual Report 2007–2008*, EgyptAir Express
2. *Annual Report 2008–2009*, EgyptAir Express
3. *Annual Report 2009–2010*, EgyptAir Express
4. *Annual Report 2006–2007*, EgyptAir Express
5. EgyptAir, eng.wikipedia.org
6. ibid
7. ibid

Chapter 13
1. Weisskopf Nora and Schlumberger CE, 'Is the Arab take-off imminent? Opportunities for the development of the North African Air Transport sector following the Arab Spring', Annals of Air and Space Law, undocs.worldbank.org, Vol. XXXVII, 2012
2. 'EgyptAir', eng.wikipedia.org

Notes and References

3. 'EgyptAir introduces the A340-200', flightglobal.com, 1 January 1997
4. 'EgyptAir gets A340 Airbus plane', upi.com, 28 November 1996
5. 'EgyptAir reaktiviert letzten A340-200', austrianwings.info, 18 February 2014
6. 'EgyptAir receives first Airbus A330-300', arabaviation.com, 30 August 2010,
7. Kaminski-Morrow, David, 'EgyptAir in talks to defer A330-300 deliveries', flightglobal.com, 1 March 2011
8. 'EgyptAir flight attendants fly with hijab for first time', egyptindependent.com, 11 November 2012
9. 'Egypt's national airline loses $185 million', gulf-daily-news.com, 16 June 2013
10. 'Nile Air', eng.wikipedia.org
11. 'Nesma Airlines', eng.wikipedia.org
12. 'Alexandria Airlines', eng.wikipedia.org
13. 'Air Italy Egypt', eng.wikipedia.org
14. 'AlMasria Universal Airlines', eng.wikipedia.org
15. 'Air Arabia', eng.wikipedia.org

Chapter 14

1. 'EgyptAir plans further restructuring as losses mount', centreforaviation.com, 15 June 2014
2. ibid
3. ibid
4. ibid
5. ibid
6. ibid
7. ibid
8. 'Russia urges tourists to avoid Egypt', moroccoworldnews.com, 15 August 2013
9. Chandler, Adam, 'How Egypt became Russia's top tourism destination', theatlantic.com, 6 November 2015
10. 'Metrojet Flight 9268', eng.wikipedia.org
11. 'EgyptAir verhandelt mit Suchoi über Superjet Bestellung', austrianwings.info, 9 July 2015
12. Flottau, Jens, 'EgyptAir Airbus A320 lost from radar over Mediterranean Sea', Air Transport World, 16 May 2016
13. Pearson, Michael, 'EgyptAir Flight 804, Conflicting reports over final moments', CNN, 1 June 2016
14. Farberov, Snejana, 'Flight that crashed and killed 66 people was caused by pilot's cigarette, investigation finds', mypost.com, 27 April 2022

Chapter 15

1. *EgyptAir Annual Report 2015–16*, EgyptAir
2. bid
3. *EgyptAir Annual Report 2016–17*, EgyptAir
4. Hofmann, Kurt, 'EgyptAir to boost Saudi Arabian network to 200 weekly flights', atwonline.com, 12 April 2016
5. Dron, Alan, 'US fines EgyptAir for Sudanese leases', atwonline.com, 11 January 2016
6. Noureddin, Old, 'EgyptAir flights to Doha hampered following diplomatic ties cut with Qatar', egyptindependent.com, 5 June 2017
7. *EgyptAir Annual Report 2016–17*, EgyptAir
8. ibid

9. ibid
10. 'EgyptAir to receive 45 new aircraft in biggest deal in its history', egyptindependent.com, 8 December 2017

Chapter 16
1. Cornwell, Alexander, 'EgyptAir to swing to a profit this year, chairman', reuters.com, 21 November 2017
2. *EgyptAir Annual Report 2017–18,* EgyptAir
3. ibid
4. 'Revamped EgyptAir duty-free shopping zones to open at TB2', timesaerospace.com, 31 May 2017
5. 'Sphinx International Airport', eng.wikipedia.org
6. 'Capital International Airport', eng.wikipedia.org
7. 'First direct flights between Cairo and Moscow resumes', indastra.com, 12 April 2018
8. Hofmann, Kurt, 'TAP Portugal, EgyptAir expand codeshare', atwonline.com, 3 April 2018
9. *EgyptAir Annual Report 2018–19,* EgyptAir
10. Ashour, Alla Ahmed, Hammoud Ghada Aly and Tawfik Hala Fouad, 'Egypt Air strategic turnaround decisions for recovery and transformation', Journal of Tourism and Sports Management, Vol.3, 2020, p256–268
11. 'Details of the restructuring project of EgyptAir and its companies', (in arabic), almalnews.com, 11 November 2019
12. Al-Awmi, Youssef, 'The completion of the incorporation of Express Air in the holding company of EgyptAir', (in arabic), almasryalyoum.com, 4 November 2019
13. 'AerCap and EgyptAir reach agreement on the leasing of two addtional Boeing 787-9 aircraft', aercap.com. press release, 18 November 2019
14. Whittle, Nick, 'EgyptAir to lease an additional two Boeing 787 Dreamliners', simpleflying.com, 18 November 2019,
15. AerCap and EgyptAir reach agreement on the conversion of seven previously executed leases for Airbus neo aircraft', aercap.com, press release, 18 November 2019
16. 'EgyptAir and Air Cairo sign codeshare agreement', timesaerospace.aero, 9 January 2020

Chapter 17
1. 'EgyptAir to receive $127.39m to weather coronavirus crisis', internationalfinance.com, 18 May 2020
2. Bailey, Joanna, 'EgyptAir seeks $185 million bailou' simpleflying.com, 16 June 2020
3. 'EgyptAir Tourism and Duty Free Co lands cloud contract with IBM', newsroom.ibm.com, 10 March 2021
4. *EgyptAir Annual Report 2019–20,* EgyptAir
5. Saied, Mohamed, 'Ghana signs joint airline deal with Egypt, bypassing Ethiopia', al-monitor.com, 27 October 2020
6. 'First EgyptAir flight between Cairo and Tel Aviv lands at Ben Gurion Airport', timesofisrael.com, 3 October 2021
7. 'EgyptAir se redresse en 2022', progres.net.eg, 26 Febuary 2022
8. Aldroubi, Mina, 'EgyptAir flight lands in Libyan capital after eight-year pause', thenationalnews.com, 10 August 2022
9. Mounir, Tarek, 'EgyptAir to train Libyan Airlines pilots', aviationsourcenews.com, 9 August 2022

Notes and References

10. 'EgyptAir cancels flights to Moscow until March 10 due to European flight insurance issue', tass.com, 5 March 2022
11. 'EgyptAir to resume daily flights to Moscow on Friday', arabnews.com, 14 April 2022
12. Osmondi, Jerry, 'EgyptAir to increase direct flights between Moscow and Sharm el Sheikh, Hurghada', africa.cgtn.com, 8 December 2022
13. 'EgyptAir to add first narrowbody freighter, a B-737-800', ch.aviation.com, 19 May 2022
14. 'Egypt's Air Cairo schedules E190 debut for late 1Q23', ch.aviation.com, 29 November 2022
15. 'Air Cairo op pad met eerste drie gehuurde E190s', pilootenvliegtuig.nl, 5 January 2023
16. Van Woerkom, Klaas Jan, 'Air Cairo op pad met ATR 72-600', luchtvaartnieuws.nl, 27 July 2022
17. Tolba, Karim, 'Egypt to launch its first low-cost carrier by late 2022', aviationbusinessme.com, 10 July 2022

Other books you might like:

Airlines Series, Vol. 9

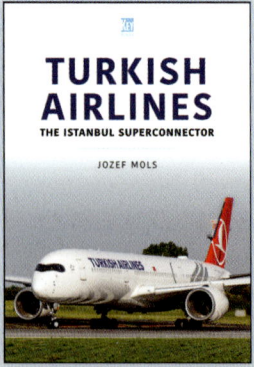
Airlines Series, Vol. 4

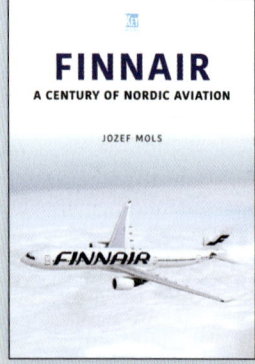
Airlines Series, Vol. 5

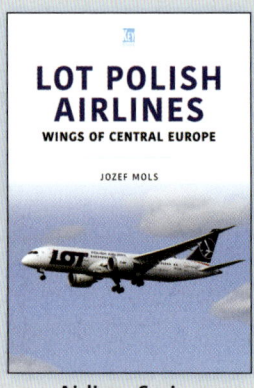
Airlines Series, Vol. 7

Airlines Series, Vol. 6

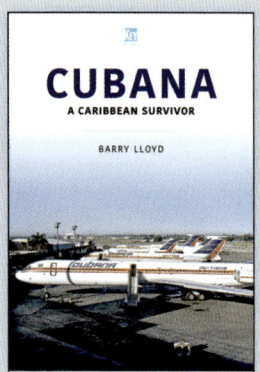
Airlines Series, Vol. 10

For our full range of titles please visit:
shop.keypublishing.com/books

VIP Book Club

Sign up today and receive
TWO FREE E-BOOKS

Be the first to find out about our forthcoming book releases and receive exclusive offers.

Register now at **keypublishing.com/vip-book-club**

Our VIP Book Club is a 100% spam-free zone, and we will never share your email with anyone else. You can read our full privacy policy at: privacy.keypublishing.com